Aspects of the Political Theory of Ayatollah Sayed Muhammad Shirazi

By

Muhammad G. Ayub

*Published by Yasin Publications with
the permission of*
Imam Shirazi World Foundation
1220 L. Street N.W. Suite # 100 – 333
Washington, D.C. 20005 – 4018,
U.S.A.
www.TheGrandAyatollah.com
English edition

Table of Contents

Table of Contents   *iii*

Foreword   *v*

Grand Ayatollah Muhammad Shirazi   *vii*

Introduction   *1*

Freedom   *2*

   The Fundamental Principle in Mankind is Freedom   **2**

   From Liberty to Liberation   **6**

   Living Manifestation   **10**

   Freedom and Social Laws   **13**

   Freedom and Oneness-of-Allah   **16**

   Conclusion   **18**

Party Organisation   *20*

   The Necessity of Organisation   **20**

   Social Development   **21**

   The Freedom of Groups   **21**

The Social Revolution   *28*

Non-Violence   *35*

   1- The Islamic Legal evidence   35

   2- The Infallible Tradition   36

   3- Sound Thought   37

   4- Experience   37

Justice   *43*

   1- The Foundation of the Islamic State.   43

   2- Equal Opportunity   44

   3- Ownership   44

   4- Redistribution of Wealth   44

   5- Criteria for the Ruler   45

Islamic Unity   *47*

   The Idea   **47**

Aspects and Fields   47
    I.   Unity of the Islamic Leadership   48
    II.   Unity of the Islamic Movement   48
    III.   Unity of the Islamic Movements   49
    IV.   Unity of Muslims (Sunni and Shi'a)   50
    V.   Unity of the Shi'a Entity   52

Methods and Tools   52

The System of Consultation (Shura)   55

Council of Religious Authorities   55

Islamic Legislative   56

Transition of the Authority to Religious Scholars   57

How Do the Religious Scholars Come to Power?   57

Method of Election   58

The Final Picture   59

An Initial Conclusion   60

Evidence of Shura (Collective Leadership) and the Final Picture 60

Elections and their Problems   62

Dilemma of the Majority Concept   64

Council of Religious Authority Faces Two Problems   65

Qualifications of the Muslim Ruler   66

Important Remarks   66

General Conclusion   67

A Quick Comparative Look   68

Foreword

As a political activist, the author of this book was fascinated by Grand Ayatollah Shirazi's views on politics and political parties, consultative system of Government and society.

It could safely be said that Grand Ayatollah Muhammad Shirazi is unique amongst Muslim religious scholars and in particular religious authorities to produce an outstanding work on such issues in terms of quality and quantity. The thoughts and ideas expressed by Ayatollah Shirazi in these works prompted the author, Muhammad Ghaleb Ayub, to compose this book to introduce the reader to those views. This book was originally published in Arabic some ten years ago. Needless to say the topic of politics and government are one of many topics covered by Ayatollah Shirazi, and since the publication date of this book in Arabic, there have been further developments and publications by Ayatollah Shirazi. At the time of writing this foreword, the list of works by Ayatollah Shirazi has topped staggering 1060 books and papers on many different subjects. Almost all of these titles are in Arabic, a few in Farsi, and only a few titles of this long list have been translated to English, as well as other languages. An outline of Ayatollah Shirazi's work and biography is presented in the following two pages.

The original book in Arabic has been translated to English by an unknown translator. The review process of this book has not been easy. This is because in checking the quotes and references given in the book, I was faced with the task of going through Ayatollah Shirazi's work in this field.

To do justice to the reader and to Ayatollah Shirazi, in order to consider further works published, I felt that another such study must be carried out. This however, would require a team of researchers to go through the great mass of Ayatollah Shirazi's work. I must confess that I was taken aback by both the enormous amount and the detailed nature of Ayatollah Shirazi's work; not only in the field of politics and associated fields but in many other domains too.

Finally, I would like to add that it was a great pleasure to have had the opportunity to be introduced to the works and thoughts of such an outstanding and uniquely eminent personality of Islam.

Dr Z. Olyabek
1st November 1999

Grand Ayatollah Muhammad Shirazi

Grand Ayatollah Muhammad Shirazi is the religious authority, *Marje'*, to millions of Muslims around the globe. A charismatic leader who is known for his high moral values, modesty and spirituality, he is a mentor and a source of aspiration to the millions; and the means of access to authentic knowledge and teachings of Islam. He has made extensive contributions in various fields of learning ranging from Jurisprudence and Theology to Politics, Economics, Law and Sociology.

Muhammad Shirazi was born in the holy city of Najaf, Iraq, in 1347 AH (Muslim calendar), 1927 AD. He belongs to a distinguished family deeply rooted in Islamic sciences, literature and virtue. The Shirazi family has produced many great scholars and *Marje'*s (a *Marje'* is the highest religious authority) as well as renowned leaders. Two of the best-known leaders are Grand Ayatollah Mirza Hassan Shirazi, leader of the constitutional "tobacco" movement in Iran and Grand Ayatollah Muhammad Taqi Shirazi, leader of the 1920 revolution in Iraq, which liberated Iraq from colonial powers. The author's father, the late Grand Ayatollah Mahdi Shirazi, has been a famous and a highly respected scholar and the *Marje'* of his time. He is a descendant of the holy prophet Muhammad peace be upon him.

Along with his father, the author settled in the holy city of Karbala, Iraq, at the age of nine. After primary education, the young Shirazi continued his studies in different branches of learning under his father's guidance as well as those of various other eminent scholars and specialists. In the course of his training he showed a remarkable talent and appetite for learning as well as a tireless commitment to his work and the cause he believed in. His extraordinary ability, and effort, earned him the recognition, by his father and other *Marje*'s and scholars, of being a *Mujtahid;* a qualified religious scholar in the sciences of Islamic jurisprudence and law. He subsequently was able to assume the office of the *Marje*' at the early age of 33 in 1960. His followers are found in many countries around the globe.

Grand Ayatollah Shirazi is distinguished for his intellectual ability and holistic vision. He is recognised for his clear ideas and realistic solutions to issues of concern to mankind. He has written various specialised studies that are considered to be among the most important references in the Islamic sciences of beliefs or doctrine, ethics, politics, economics, sociology, law, human rights, etc. He has enriched the world with his staggering contribution of some 980 books, treatise and studies on various branches of learning. His works range from simple introductory books for the young generations to literary and scientific masterpieces. Deeply rooted in the holy Qur'an and the Teachings of the Prophet of Islam, his vision and theories cover areas such as Politics, Economics, Government, Management, Sociology, Theology, Philosophy, History and Islamic Law. His work on Islamic Jurisprudence (*al-Fiqh* series) for example constitutes 150 volumes, which run into more than 55,000 pages. Through his original thoughts and ideas he has championed the causes of issues such as the family, human right, freedom of expression, political pluralism, non-violence, and *Shura* or consultative system of leadership.

Grand Ayatollah Shirazi believes in the fundamental and elementary nature of freedom in mankind. He calls for freedom of expression, political plurality, debate and discussion, tolerance and forgiveness. He strongly believes in the consultative system of leadership and calls for the establishment of the leadership council of religious authorities. He calls for the establishment of the universal Islamic government to encompass all the Muslim countries. These and other ideas are discussed in detail in his books.

As a leader of the worldwide Muslim community, Grand Ayatollah Shirazi has always opposed despotism. In 1971 he was exiled to Lebanon by the Ba'thist regime of Iraq. He later stayed in Kuwait until 1979 when he migrated to the holy city of Qum, Iran.

Ayatollah Shirazi has established many Islamic centres, medical and financial institutions, educational, welfare and social foundations, libraries and *Hawzah's*, or universities for Islamic Sciences, in different regions of the world. These institutions are found in Australia, India, Pakistan, Afghanistan, Iran, Iraq, Kuwait, UAE, Qatar, Syria, Britain, Denmark, Sweden, Canada and USA.

Hundreds of individuals have graduated from his school as scholars, lecturers, authors and researchers.

x

Introduction

An original thinker is one who enjoys a number of characteristics, the most important of which are;

- Possession of a cosmic and general vision of existence,
- Realistic treatment of life in the light of the ideology adopted,
- Presentation of the view on the basis of reason.

Grand Ayatollah Muhammad Shirazi is one such thinker who is in possession of all three dimensions. This may be due to a personal talent, but there is no doubt that it is a gift from Islam, which he embraces, advocates and defends.

Islam is the cosmic, universal, realistic religion that bases its evidence on reason. It is only natural that such important qualities leave their impact on the thoughts, ideas and behaviour of every believer in this religion. Anyone who reads Shirazi's works would come to this conclusion. Shirazi talks of life and its problems in the language of the ideological theorist, not that of a poet or a reformist, nor that of a passer-by. He distances himself from the dialectic and adopts a style of debate. He always stresses that his main objective is to involve the reader in the topic he is writing on.

His writings are distinct for the great detail of evidence and successive proofs he offers, even when discussing the simplest of issues, whether in their defence or against them. Shirazi's researches and studies are aimed at reshaping man and history, boldly and confidently, in the light of what he has adopted.

It is worth mentioning here that, in his thoughts, Ayatollah Shirazi always places concerns of life as his top priority. That is why his writings on jurisprudence, freedom, economics, sociology, politics and constitution are more in quantity and deeper in content and quality than with other issues. That is how we can explain the practical and realistic dimension of Shirazi's thought and concern.

It is hoped that this book will provide the reader with some ideas about the main dimensions of Shirazi's thoughts and visions.

Freedom

The Fundamental Principle in Mankind is Freedom

Every theory must have a strong foundation to stand on, be it an ideological interpretation of things, or a scientific explanation of cosmic or social and psychological happenings. Such a foundation is the starting point for the researcher or the ideologist, which forms the basis for him to create and develop his vision.

There can be no doubt that such strong foundation would reflect positively on the ideas emanating from and based on it. It is the same kind of relation we always find between the root and the branch; the foundation and the edifice, even between cause and effect - to use philosophical terminology.

There is no doubt, either, that the critical process in its constructive and de-constructive forms is related to and dependent on, from the very beginning and both in the planning and execution stages, the test that the foundation is subjected to, and on the testing of the foundations against the values of analytical and values based intellect. The choice of the basis on which a theory is established is the logical and practical standing point in the process of analysing the theory or studying it.

Critics of Marxism have got used to addressing their criticism of this school by analysing the foundation, i.e. the idea of anti-thesis. Why? Because it is the spirit that reverberates throughout all the constituents of Marxist ideology, and in every aspect of that ideology; be it concerned with the explanation of the cosmos or the analysis of the historical march of the human society throughout its long history, or with social education which this ideology holds as the final solution of all human problems.

It is usual for critics of metaphysical theories to direct their strongest attacks against the principle of causality, as it is the basis of all metaphysical thought when presenting a holistic picture of existence, its origin, its motion and its direction.

We have made this introduction, long as it is, in order to say that Ayatollah Shirazi has a theoretical attitude towards freedom.

He discusses this civilised value as a person who believes in and interacts with it; he sometimes defines it as if he were deeply in love with it. On occasions, he pursues it seeking its spiritually reviving touch; yet in the end Ayatollah Shirazi is none but a committed ideologist with a vision that is total and integral.

Before stating the details of his vision we may ask what is the basis of Shirazi's theoretical concept of freedom? In a word it is "fundamentalism". It is the innate originality of freedom. Mankind is created and moulded to be free. Freedom is not something that can be given or gained; it is simply a necessity.

Shirazi: *"The Fundamental Principle in Mankind is Freedom"*[1].

Thus we see in this statement the beginnings of an institution, a pure theoretical basis, and an abstraction, whose advocate puts forward his theory of freedom. He gives examples from real life, physical and tangible presence. He deals with the questions, philosophically, yet in the language of the truthful which clarifies the real meaning. In his detailed commentary of Sabzawari's long epic poem, Ayatollah Shirazi states:

"The articulate self is an active being willingly and by inspiration: It uses its powers and creates images deep inside its existence. The self, therefore, imagines, incline towards - or away from - things, and contemplates and meditates."[2] To that he adds, ".. By stating that the self is a premeditating agent, this is so because man moves according to knowledge, will and intention..." [3].

The word 'moves' used above is to express day-to-day life experience in a broad sense, yet man may be forced to do certain things! Man may even do something as an expression of a natural, innate instructs!

To these two problematic questions Shirazi answers as follows:

---

[1] M. Shirazi, *al-Fiqh* series, volume 101, Politics, p 63

[2] M. Shirazi, "Commentary on Sabzewari", page 308

[3] ibid.. p 310

"Every doer - even instinctively - entails a purpose, an aim..." [4]. Even a stone, when it falls from above, does so. Consequently, "the use of force is not an on-going phenomenon, nor is it frequent. In fact compulsion is a rarity and should never be a pretext to negate the above-mentioned totality"[5]. I.e., free action and free acts, and, consequently, free life emanating from the innate originality of freedom, even if we were flexible on the issue of a purpose "and its relation to acts, even forced ones" [6].

In accordance with the above, mankind is free; his freedom emanates from the self, from within, from the depth of his innate self.

Yet, what basis does Shirazi have, on which he builds this foundation?

As a matter of fact, conscience does confirm man's freedom. This is the method Islamic philosophers use to prove and confirm the originality of freedom in this, most revered being. Yet, because Shirazi is an Islamic theoretician defending a precise and definite viewpoint, he falls back on the Qur'an and the Prophet's tradition (Sunnah) when seeking proof of this innate originality. That is why he included one whole chapter titled "Clauses on Freedom" [7] in one of his books, in order to discuss and explain that originality.

Some of these clauses are:

1. *"Never be someone else's slave, whereas Allah has made you Free."*
2. *"People are all free."*

Both statements are by Ali [8] peace be upon him. The first statement embodies the fundamental aspect of freedom, perfectly and uniquely skilfully because it means:

---

[4] ibid.. p 311

[5] ibid.. p 311

[6] ibid. p 20

[7] M. Shirazi, "The New Order for the World of Faith, Freedom, Prosperity and Peace", p31

[8] Ali ibn Abi-Talib, the cousin and the son-in-law of the Prophet of Islam, Muhammad, peace be upon them.

- Freedom is a fundamental right and innate to mankind,
- Freedom is not an external addendum but a divine creation.

This cosmic freedom is what mankind is born with. But this innate and essentially deep-rooted freedom in man is not a mere capability to choose from a number of options or alternatives.

In most of the western literature freedom is projected as an abstract capability. In fact, this capability has the highest priority on the list of this natural value of the human being.

Freedom, within the limits of available choice, reflects its first primitive stage. This is what "comes to our minds when we imagine ourselves free" [9].

But there are higher and more sublime degrees of freedom, in the shape of its movements and activities. There is what some researchers describe as 'the freedom of subjective independence' which means 'actions guided by thinking and calculation' i.e. acting through a feeling of responsibility, or responsible action [10]. There is also 'The freedom of perfection', which advocates emancipation from all forms of personal (or self-imposed) bounds and restrictions such as desires, instincts and ignorance. Philosophers like Spinoza, Lenths and the Greek philosophers have emphasised this type of freedom. [11]

Last but not least, there is the 'freedom of the Self', which, in short, means the permanent awareness of the self or the personality of the being. The French philosopher Bergson is foremost amongst the theoreticians of this type of freedom.

All these definitions, derivations and subsidiaries, even if true, are in fact none but a mere reflection of the fundamental and innate nature of freedom, and, thus, of its first order i.e. the abstract capability to choose. Were it not for this principle, the possibility of perfection and the capability to perform calculated actions would be non-existent. These

---

[9] Z. Ibrahim, "The problem of Freedom", p 20

[10] ibid. p 21

[11] ibid.

are only the consequences of freedom; they are not freedom in its essence and principle.

In his theory of freedom, Shirazi defines all those forms as activities of the human self.

Mankind is able to create mental ideas and images; and after the process of thinking and calculation he can act. He yearns for perfection because he is a purposeful creature.

'Purpose' is related to free-will antecedents, as much as to past experience of relatively precise and accurate depictions that varies from one person to another. It is equally related to a choice that is both contemplative and calculated. Shirazi states:

"Every doer - even doers by natural instinct - must entail a purpose or an aim. The man, who walks, seeks a purpose, i.e., meeting a friend etc. The cause of purposefulness has an entity, and an identity, which is the cause of the actions of the doer. Also, the very presence of a purpose is the very object of the actions of the doer. Thus, the purpose is the cause of the motion of a doer in the direction of the act."[12]. A human being, therefore, acts and moves for a purpose, which means that purpose is the cause of his motion, which, in turn, requires predetermined thought and calculation, as well as self-awareness.

The type of freedom presented by western philosophic thought stems from man's free exercise and practice. This exercise and practice does happen by direct action emanating from this creature. Any human being can classify this free exercise under several categories, yet that has no influence on the process of classifying or categorising freedom in its essential meaning, i.e. its Islamic meaning, into kinds and types.

That is why the western effort in this respect is an addendum to clarify, rather than addition to the essence.

From Liberty to Liberation

---

[12] M. Shirazi, "Commentary on Sabzewari", page 312

The discussion above, which has been detailed in full, centres on freedom at the principle level, i.e. in its philosophical aspect related to the human entity, that is whether man is free or not?

For there have emerged a number of theories proposed by human thought to the effect that man is 'destined' or 'forced' to do every action he does, that he has no free will in the world of action or movement or even imagination. Such theories have had their ill effect on the history of mankind. They have led man, directly and indirectly, to submit and surrender to oppression and tyranny. They have frozen and immobilised his spirit of movement and initiative.

Against those theories has stood firm the school of freedom which views man as a contemplating, intellectual and an active energy.

We have presented the theory of Shirazi on this issue. We have seen that he is one of the supporters of "freedom", i.e. one of those who believe that man has the power to choose from the options and alternatives. He believes that man is a purposeful being, acting according to a calculated will, well aware of a clear and defined objective.

It is quite clear that freedom in this sense is outside the bounds and scope of the discussion of any school of thought. Its qualities do not belong to any particular school of thought. For it is Allah's gift to mankind; it is not a gift of any particular school of thought so that it can be studied on a basis of that thought[13]. Yet there is no doubt that freedom in this sense is inseparable from social freedom. That is, the issue that freedom is conferred upon man by a certain social school of thought in order to exercise life, and the battle to prove whether freedom is innate and original or not, are within the scope of pure philosophical thought. While the struggle to provide the opportunities of life are within the scope of social thought. It seems that the issue that has concerned mankind and the various nations, and which still reaps fear and panic in the hearts of people is the freedom in its practical and applied dimension.

Freedom, which has been used as a pretext for bloodshed and violation of all individuals, and which has been used as an excuse to restrict freedom itself, is none but social freedom. In the name of that freedom, and under its banner, rivers of blood were shed in Europe; the French

---

[13] M.B. Sadr, "Our Economics", volume 1, p 282.

revolution is but an example. In the name of freedom people were forbidden from expressing their very existence, thought and civilisation; the socialist bloc states after World War II are one example. In the name of that freedom the class system was created, and so were its fatal bounds which have ever since paralysed the will of the majority, and let loose the will of the elite minority in the capitalist states.

Political battles have been fought for social freedom but never for the belief in the freedom vis-à-vis predestination of man. History, however, is not totally devoid of such battles for that belief.

Despite all this, we cannot deny the relation between the principle basis of freedom - as an essential value in mankind and a basic constituent of his very existence, and the practical nature of freedom. Yet we stress, at the same time, the fact that battles for freedom throughout history have embodied, first and foremost, social freedom. What value would individuals have, even though freedom is fundamental, if continued endeavours are made to block mankind's chances of honourable and honest life?

And what value is there in all theorisations in defence of the originality of human freedom, while it is being suppressed in real life?

That is why Lisson says, "Freedom is inseparable and an indivisible part of the will to be free" [14].

And Marcelle is quoted to say:

"Existence, value and freedom are so inter-related that they can be saved only together" [15].

The essence of all such ideas is the existence and confirmation *of freedom as action, freedom as an event* and *freedom as a practical experience.*

This issue is what some authors probably refer to within the context of the well-known slogan (*from liberty to liberation*), or from liberties to liberation.

---

[14] Z. Ibrahim, "The Problem of Freedom", p 198

[15] ibid.. p 199

Liberation as a philosophy does not aim at proving that the human being is free, rather, it endeavours to illustrate how man can be more liberated.

Here lies the problem or the riddle of mankind, regimes, history, religion, rulers and society.

In his discussions on freedom, Shirazi concentrates on this issue in remarkably great detail. On the practical side of freedom, he goes as far as to link the issues and facts related to freedom. Why? Is it to clarify a misunderstanding that no freedom exists in Islam? Is it a personal and psychological yearning for work? Or is it a drive to discuss crucial issues of concern to mankind?

All these answers are possible, but not enough to cover that unusual interest in social freedom, his main concern and mental obsession, which his pen deals with every so often.

Obviously, Shirazi goes into great detail when he talks of freedom, because it is an essential value in the doctrine or ideology which he embraces, namely Islam. Combined with this is his personal vitality as seen in the quantity of his writings and his relentless political activity.

In any case, Ayatollah Shirazi speaks of 'social freedom' as an essential and prominent element of his political theory. There is no doubt that his ideological and social Islamic background has played a great part in forming this tendency in him; his vitality and experience have played another role in this respect. Hence Shirazi's usually bitter talks on dictatorship. For, he who reads Shirazi's works on injustice, tyranny and oppression will feel the author's pure spirit and emotions, and understand, instinctively, the extent to which he benefits from a liberated spirituality.[16]

Now back to our main issue...

The move from liberties to liberation is the crux of the matter in the case of freedom, and has ever been since man became aware of his existence. Through his theses, Shirazi emphasises the fact that such a move is one of the main legislative adoptions of Islam.

---

[16] M. Shirazi, "The Way to Muslim Revival", pp 344-346

To that effect he states that, "Given that mankind being free, Freedom is a fact; without chaos and without suppression - explicit or implicit - and it does not exist but in the Islamic systems." [17]

Once this fundamental theory is established, Shirazi moves on to the practical details:

"In Islam (exists) doctrinal liberation, economic liberation, political liberation, cultural (intellectual) liberation, and social liberation". [18]

Such is the general picture...
Freedom is a natural reality in mankind, a subjective reality. Liberation is the practical side of this freedom and Islam emphasises the fundamental nature of freedom.

Islam approves of liberation.

Consequently, the theory develops into its general structural form.

Hence the well-known slogan: There is no freedom without liberation... There is no liberation without freedom.

Living Manifestation

We are still discussing the general outlines. Freedom is innate and fundamental to mankind. Liberation is the tangible material form of this originality. But where does the evidence of freedom lie? More precisely: where do we find liberation?

To this very delicate and testing question, Shirazi answers by giving practical evidence. He gives us a hundred examples of the freedom legislated by Islam. Of these are "the freedom of worship, of selling, of buying, of mortgage, of security, of invention, of giving bonds, of reconciliation, of insurance, of companies, of transaction, of agriculture, of water-irrigation, of land ownership, of deposits, of property leases, of renting and letting, of power of attorney, of giving, of giving alms, of giving gifts, of inhabiting, of building, of running races, of throwing

---

[17] ibid. p 341

[18] ibid.

10

arrows, of making wills, of getting married, of getting divorced, of having divorce by mutual consent, of breast feeding, of travelling, of stay, of opening a shop, of putting rewards, of printing, of taking a profession, of having education and culture, of making a pledge, of making an oath, of dedication, of land reclamation, of agricultural cultivation, of creating industries, of construction, of publishing a commercial newspaper, of owning a broadcasting station and T.V. station, of forming political parties, organisations and societies, of establishing trade unions, of enjoying the freedom of belief, etc."[19]

Some may be surprised at this long list of types of freedom, which Shirazi presents to us. But such astonishment is irrelevant, for many reasons:

1. The list is a true and real expression of the totality of freedom in the Islamic system, and an embodiment of the unlimited Islamic attitude towards exercising freedom on the widest scale possible. In communist countries, freedom has neither an existence nor a trace... Liberties existent in the so-called free world amount to a small fraction of those granted by Islam. The 'free world' countries have no freedom of letting, construction, industry, agriculture, commerce or ownership. Man has no freedom if he is tied by passports, identity cards, nationality and the like." [20]

2. A great injustice is inflicted on Islamic law when it is accused of oppression, suppression, despotism and coercion. Indeed, it is the body of laws that incorporates the greatest number of evidences of social freedom. By producing such a list, Shirazi provides the tangible proof of that, and equally strongly refutes the false allegations and accusations against Islam.

In fact, this list of freedoms in Islam can be classified in the following general categories:

I.   Intellectual and ideological freedoms
II.   Social freedom
III.   Political freedom
IV.   Economic freedom

---

[19] ibid.

[20] ibid. pp 316-321

But Ayatollah Shirazi re-asserts intellectual freedom far more than the others. He believes that this freedom develops man and society, and makes history. In particular, he emphasises one aspect of that freedom; the freedom of expression. To emphasise its importance he submits four reasons.

Because freedom of writing reveals the weak and wrong sides of policies of a certain regime. It is the means to educate the nation on a sound basis. Its absence means suppression which leads to explosions; and, finally, because freedom of expression is what deters rulers from committing tyranny and warns them against dictatorship." [21]

Shirazi's highest score is his evaluation of the freedom of thought when he emphatically and boldly states that freedom of expression is not subjected to any restrictions or limits. All the restrictions and limits such freedom may have or have not lie in the boundary of harm. That is to say, limits here are of a passive or negative nature; when freedom takes the form of looting, for example, it should be stopped. But who decides what "harm" justifies denying such freedom or suspending it? To that Shirazi answers as follows:
"The useful and the harmful are matters of convention (or common sense), like all conventional issues." [22]

This is a remarkable thought, combining freedom with convention. It is, (the combination) a practical method of solving a tricky obstacle, usually raised by advocates of absolute freedom, which is really nothing but chaos.

In its practical forms, freedom is never divorced from the movement and activities of life to which society is accustomed. Conventional values are in fact the conscience of a community, both doctrinal (ideological) and educational, especially if emanating from an education approved by Islam. Clear conscience and standards of serious progress, and the harmful and the useful are all practical issues formulated in the shape of convention on the basis of samples of acceptable behaviour. In the light of conventional values man's behaviour and actions are defined. Shirazi goes on to say that:

---

[21] M. Shirazi, *al-Fiqh* series, volume 101, Politics pp 220-222

[22] ibid. p 223

"If controversy arises concerning the validity of a certain proof, the Judiciary are the final authority, and there is the final word of probity and fairness." [23]

This is in fact another reference to the conscience of the community; for the Judiciary, especially in Islamic Law, embodies the spirit of the community in as much as that community accepts its legislation, rules standards and values. Reference to Judicial authority is in fact a reference and endorsement of an interpretation unanimously approved by the will of the community. We are, thus, witnessing a process of modern interactive and enriching combination of freedom, convention and legislation.

Shirazi's concern in the freedom of expression is far greater than his interest in other freedoms because of the importance of that particular freedom in the formation of man, and in guiding the process of a good political regime.

There is no doubt that intellectual freedom, or the freedom of expression, is a theoretical starting point for all other types of freedom. That is why despotic regimes fear intellectual freedom far more than any other freedom. Through intellectual freedom, a society can march along pioneering paths of life on all levels and in every aspect. Intellectual freedom comes first.

We can say, therefore, that one of the basics of Shirazi's vision of freedom is the top priority of intellectual freedom. This is not because of any procedural or legal order of priority, but because of the innate importance of the manifestation of freedom, and because all manifestations of freedom are a coherent texture of values and rights.

Freedom and Social Laws

There is no doubt that a complicated relationship exists between freedom and social laws. Some intellectuals are of the opinion that laws are responsible for defining and limiting freedom; or, laws are responsible for guiding and maintaining freedom. In fact it is not easy to

---

[23] ibid.

define such responsibilities and it is no secret that there are stark differences between 'defining – limiting' and 'guiding – maintaining'.

Whatever the attitude towards such terms (definition-limit; guidance-maintenance) may be, the common characteristics of all these remains the rule of law, in one form or another, over freedom.

The result of all that is that the law is the basis, the essence, while freedom is a secondary issue; the law is the framework that controls freedom.

Naturally, such an attitude contradicts and denies the sanctity and importance of freedom in life, and denies the fact that freedom is the basis or the essence. But does that mean ignoring the role of law?

The law is also a necessity. There is no longer an urgent need to prove the utmost importance of law to man, especially in developed and sophisticated societies. We have never been in circumstances that would make it incumbent on us to prove the failure of the theory of chaos, which denies both the states and the law.

In this respect, Shirazi formulates an opinion, which is almost unique. He is a pioneering advocate of freedom; intellectual freedom in particular, yet he states that it is the social law that ought to be within the framework of freedom and controlled by it.

Formulating laws according to and within the framework of freedom is a bold and revolutionary idea dealing with the depiction of the relationship between laws and freedom.

Laws do not rule freedom; it is freedom that rules laws. This is an attractive pioneering human thought.
Imam Shirazi is of the opinion that it is necessary "for the two authorities, the legislative and the executive, to emanate from human freedom." [24]
Reversing the formula would better clarify the idea: Freedom is what formulates the law; the law does not formulate freedom. Why? Shirazi

---

[24] M. Shirazi, *al-Fiqh* series, volume 101, Politics p 24

gives more than one reason why this is so, but the most important one is that, "The fundamental principle in mankind is Freedom." [25]

It is on this basis that the relationship between freedom and social laws is defined. Whenever most legislators want to present or form a law, they first think of a situation in which chaos or irresponsible freedom would prevail. Laws, therefore, must be made to define or deny the freedom of each and every individual. In Islam, however, it is freedom that formulates the pictures of life and society. And naturally such freedom should be sensible and responsible.

Shirazi's theory follows a clear method, not a vague or ambiguous one. An important question is bound to arise in this concern: How do social laws emanate from freedom?

Freedom, in this sense, is action, exercise or practice, and a real tangible happening. Shirazi believes that freedom in this respect is in the best interest of the community as embodied by Islam. The interest and welfare of the nation is guaranteed in Islam, and it is Islam that formulates life itself.

Indeed, if we reviewed the examples presented by Shirazi of the manifestation of freedom in Islam, we easily discover this fact. Islam allows the enjoyment of life in its broadest meanings. Such allowance is what defines and limits:

- Everything is clean and pure for man unless otherwise proven,
- Everything is allowed unless otherwise proven,
- In principle, everything is allowed in Islam.
- No one may harm or be harmed in Islam,
- "And in Islam, too, ... There is cultural liberation: Every man has the right to attain whatever knowledge and education he wishes to achieve. No obstacle, be it money or anything else, should prevent him from going to university and beyond" [26]
- "Social liberation or freedom is also part of Islam, where there are no class concessions, usually protected by laws discriminating

---

[25] ibid. p 240

[26] ibid.

between nationalities, ethnic backgrounds, languages, colours and regional affiliations" [27]

A comprehensive and deep reading into these statements and their wording, be it in the starting points, the consequences or the contents would lead to the important conclusion that it is freedom that decides the form of law, and not vice versa.
There is freedom on the move . . .
There is allowing on the move . . .
But freedom restricts itself when it turns into harm, for 'harm' is not one of the components of freedom, nor of its requirements; it is only a whimsical addendum to it... 'Restriction' here is not exactly the semantic meaning of the word; rather, it is a kind of safeguarding the value, an innate, subjective safeguard emanating from within.

Freedom here means lifting of restrictions. Laws are derived from it, hence the words of Allah the Almighty:

"That He may relieve them of their pain, and the chains that were inflicted upon them..." [28]
And

"No coercion in faith; Right is distinct from Wrong" [29]
And verse
"You have your religion; I have mine" [30]

All these verses give freedom priority over law as a civilised, intellectual, political and social value. Then comes the Law, in accordance with this freedom.

Freedom and Oneness-of-Allah

Ayatollah Shirazi relates freedom to the Oneness of Allah (one of the basic principles of Islam). He states:

---

[27] ibid.

[28] The holy Qur'an, The Heights (7): 157

[29] The holy Qur'an, The Cow (2): 256

[30] The holy Qur'an, The Unbelievers (109): 6

"He who thinks deeply of the words 'there is no god but Allah' - which are repeated in the Qur'an and the Teaching (of the Prophet of Islam) thousands of times and quoted by Muslims in their prayers and other rites - will find in these words the symbol and essence of freedom. The Persian emperors were considered gods, and offspring of deity; they would inflict death or give life, just like the Roman emperors, who were also considered gods, whose disobedience was like disobeying god himself. Christians mention in their Holy books the rule: what belongs to Caesar is Caesar's; what belongs to god is god's). Religion is for god; life is for Caesar and the priests in Europe and elsewhere. Those considered themselves mediators -middlemen- between god and people.

They claimed that they had in their possession the authority to send whomever they wanted to Paradise, or to Hell.

That was the case, too, with the Buddhists in India and China. So did others, like the Israelites, who said to Moses (PBUH):

"Make us a god, like the gods they have" [31]

Even stones became gods amongst Arabs and non-Arabs, complete with servants and clergy. Void traditions and superstitions had their strong influence on man. Even today, there are millions of idols in India, China and Japan. In the communist countries we find human idols, like Lenin, Marks and others. Before the advent of Islam, mankind was, and still is today, succumbed under the yoke of thousands of restrictions, chains and slavery in many countries. When the last messenger of Allah, Muhammad, declared his motto: *"There is no god but Allah"*, he in fact declared an all-out war on all those chains and restrictions. His declaration is that there is none but only one master in this world, Allah is Almighty. Only Allah must be obeyed. Every man can establish a direct contact with Allah.

As for the prophets and the impeccable Imams (leaders appointed by the prophets (PBUT)), they are the ambassadors of Revelation, who convey Allah's principles to mankind.

A book by a western author, which was translated into Arabic under the title "The heritage of Persia", states that kings of ancient Persia were the closest creatures to god, and whenever people spoke to the king, they would not mention his name, but say instead "You, the Deity". The

---

[31] The holy Qur'an, The Heights (7): 138

17

religion of the Zoroastrian conferred divinity on the kings; their orders were sacred, their offspring were above mankind and their rule was that of god.

The same phenomenon was prevalent with all other rulers before Islam; they called their kings "*Rabb*" (god, lord). When the Persian Emperor sent two men to kill the messenger of Allah (PBUH), and to carry his severed head to their king, the messenger found that they had shaven their beards and twisted their moustaches. He asked, "Who ordered you to do this"? "Our Rabb" they answered, meaning, of course, their Persian king. The Messenger then said, "But my Rabb has ordered me to keep my beard and shorten my moustache". Then he added, "My Rabb (god) has killed your Rabb (king)".

In this and similar hadiths (traditions) we find reference to kings as " Rabbs", just to bring the meaning close to their minds.

Even in the Holy Qur'an we read that Jews and Christians called their prophets sons of god, and sometimes, His partners; and that they called their priests and clergy by the same names Rabbi's).[32]

The relation, therefore, between Oneness of Allah and freedom is an innate one. The stronger the belief in the oneness of Allah in the mind of man, the stronger his awareness of freedom, which he then exercises and applies with vehemence in its widest sense.

Therefore "Oneness is the symbol of freedom"[33], according to Shirazi, yet this symbol is neither a mark nor a sign; it is simply a real fact.

Conclusion

Shirazi's theory of freedom can, therefore, be summarised in the following points: -

1. Freedom is innate - fundamental nature in man
2. Liberation is the practical manifestation of freedom in real life

---

[32] M. Shirazi, "The New Order for the World of Faith, Freedom, Prosperity and Peace", pp 314-316

[33] ibid.

3. Islam combines together the innateness of freedom and the necessity for liberation
4. It is freedom that defines social laws
5. The relation between freedom and Oneness (of God) is an essential one.

Party Organisation

Ayatollah Shirazi discusses political party organisation in the context of his general political philosophy derived from Islamic principles. This is why he does not refer to this type of organisation in a language of total approval or total rejection. He draws support from a number of supporting evidence.

The Islamic political vision of Shirazi is based on the Islamic concept of leadership council of religious authorities, (Shirazi calls for the establishment of the consultative system of leadership), as well as on freedom, social progress and political plurality. All of these criteria help adept party activities, but only according to their own statutory terms and conditions.

Shirazi's views on the freedom of political parties are based upon civilisation and social progress. Most important of those basics are:

The Necessity of Organisation

Shirazi is of the opinion that organisation should be the solid grounds of every purposeful action. This is because organisation is:[34]

I.   A "duty" according to Ali (PBUH) who says,
        "To you I recommend fear of Allah, and the organisation of your affairs"
II.   A "cosmic order", according to the Qur'anic Verse: *".. of everything... measured"*
III.   A "vital need, and a source of strength", according to the Qur'anic Verse:
        "Prepare for them all (sorts) of strengths you can"

On this basis Shirazi calls for resorting to organisation in order to perform the doctrinal, political and economic roles. This basis is only second to awareness, in the process of creating vigilance amongst the Muslims. There is no doubt that the "party" is at the highest level of organisation and one of the most authentic turning points of organised action.

---

[34] M. Shirazi, "The Way to Muslim Revival", p 57

Social Development

Shirazi believes in the need for social development, and that a political party can play such a role. "As for 'the party' in the political sense of the word, it is part of the community, whose aim is to push the nation forward, to reform corruption, and to help avert danger. It is, therefore, part of this nation. It is distinguished by its organisation, its deeper understanding of the situation, and the greater volume of action... It is of the nation and for the nation. If it comes to power it gives wider services and reforms: and since the party is part of the nation it services the whole nation. It speaks of the nation as a whole, and struggles to come to power for the sake of that whole..."[35] Shirazi, thus, believes in the freedom of party activity, because it is a means of development.

The Freedom of Groups

This is another basis on which Shirazi relies in adopting freedom of political actions based on party organisation, for a party is a kind of gathering, but with a specific aim and disciplined.

To that effect he says, "The state has no right to forbid mass-meeting or gathering, whether temporary for celebration, condolences, or exchange of views; or permanent, as in the case of forming societies, trade unions, committees and the like... because of the fundamental nature of human freedom."[36]

This total concept of freedom according to Shirazi no doubt leads to this conclusion within the framework of political action.

The fact of the matter is that such basics have civilised dimensions. Hence the very special views of Shirazi on the organisations that truly and rightly fit this description. A party cannot be called one unless it acquires the following characteristics:

1. To aim at coming to power

---

[35] M. Shirazi, *al-Fiqh* series, volume 102, Politics, p 110

[36] M. Shirazi, *al-Fiqh* series, volume 106, Politics, p 226

2. To identify with the masses, for a party must "establish the closest of ties with the masses, which is what enables the party to expand, quantitatively as well as qualitatively, and to score successes."[37]

3. To have internal organisation and constitution: for, "a party is not merely external entity; it is a philosophy that draws its members closer together, and defines its aims and means"[38]

4. Continuous work, activity and giving for "a party must always be an ever flowing waterfall. It is the duty of a party to keep the momentum of unrelenting activity."[39]

5. Expansion by means of "local organisations and institutions which will be linked to the central nucleus of the party"[40]

6. To have a firm organisation, for "the organisation should be (of) iron"[41] Yet this strict party discipline must be coupled with the "freedom of the grass root"[42].

Such equation can be achieved, Shirazi believes, by observing two conditions:

A. Total and complete obedience to the leadership, with conviction,

B. The grass root should elect the leadership.[43]

Only thus can the organisation maintain its cohesion, inter-action and unity. This is the best formula ever coined by theoreticians and leaders of organised movements, for it combines indispensable necessities and requirements.

7. Appealing to masses: for, "all the party's institutions and members must be one with the masses, channelling their energies and leading

---

[37] ibid., p 104

[38] ibid., p 102

[39] ibid., p 104

[40] ibid.

[41] M. Shirazi, "The Way to Muslim Revival", pp77-78

[42] ibid.

[43] ibid.

them in the battles of liberation from colonialism and oppression".[44]

Shirazi sets two conditions for the party to be described as the party of the masses:

A. Honest leadership
B. Respect for the masses

To be a popular party, by applying these two conditions, is a basic requirement in any contemporary organisational ideology.

8. To respond to the masses' needs: by "rendering services to the masses and endeavouring to win their support".[45] Commenting on the importance of this point Shirazi states that "appealing to the masses is a difficult task, but has a praiseworthy outcome. The difficulty lies in the fact that the masses have needs, and if an organisation does not meet those needs, it soon loses the masses; and subsequently the organisation's demise becomes inevitable"[46]

9. Consultative system (Shura): "A party must be based on consultation, never on self-opinionated despotism. Wherever consultation has been applied to any matter, it has produced progress and prosperity"[47]

10. Vigilance: No organisation has the right to put itself forward as a political party unless it plays this effective role. "..It is necessary for all party activists to provide comprehensive and deep awareness for the party members in order to understand the world and the religion. It is important for a party to be aware of what is going on around it, in which case it becomes a strong and steadfast organisation...."[48]

The above are the basic indicators considered by Shirazi to be essential in any party organisation if it wants to be worthy of this political

---

[44] ibid.

[45] ibid., p 93

[46] ibid., p 69

[47] ibid.

[48] ibid., 74-75

support. If we study them well we find they contain the following aspects:

- Objectives: coming to power, leading the nation, change and development;
- Means and tools: contact with the masses, awareness, meeting the masses' needs,
- General qualities of a party: Articles of Association, Consultation, discipline, continuous winning.

According to this vision, a party is a civilised and organised institution that with its ideological programme actively moves forward to achieve its aims. The important basis in a party is not only the inner structure[49] or the struggle as a first and ultimate fact, or the revolutionary activity alone; rather, it is all those factors working together in harmony. There can be no party without a theory; no theory without embodying action; and no embodying action without contact with the masses... All these issues embody the party in the real political sense of the word.

Based on this vision, Shirazi's opinion is that parties have an effective role to play in the movement of history, for they

1. Help select the best
2. Contribute to the will of the nation winning the upper hand
3. Create political awareness amongst the masses
4. Bear the political responsibilities
5. Help establish the intellectual and political discipline in the nation
6. Encourage creative competition
7. Pushes the society forward[50]

But this does not mean that party activity is free of shortcomings. It may bring untoward and grave consequences to the political life of the nation, the people and the society. Of such consequence are dictatorship, showing hostility, distorting facts, etc. Yet all these shortcomings give no evidence to support any view forbidding or rejecting the philosophy of party activity. It is no secret that every social structure has its own negative and positive characteristics; it is the winning of one over the other that entails the suitable stance. To this effect Shirazi states that "...

---

[49] The Psychology of Politics

[50] M. Shirazi, *al-Fiqh* series, volume 102, Politics, Article 37, pp127-137

For everything proved to have useful and harmful sides, if these equalise or one side wins over the other to such an extent that neutralises it, one such side is ruled permitted (*halaal*) or forbidden (*haraam*)"[51]

He then lists the harmful sides and the response to them:

1. A party undermines the freedom of a member belonging to its organisational, political and activist circle. Shirazi believes this criticism to be irrelevant, for a man who decides to identify with and belong to (a party) does that freely and willingly. If a majority decision is adopted, it is because it is an implementation of the general or majority will, which is bound to be beneficial to that individual"[52]

2. A party splits the unity of the nation. This, Shirazi states, depends on the party's education and the qualities of its activists, and the extent of the nation's vigilance, as well as on the number of parties in the field. It has nothing to do with the ideology of party activity as a philosophy, method, and way. The opposite sometimes happens, for as, when sound party activity is available, it may lead to the unity of the nation's will. The cause of the creation is always an effect that is consistent with itself.

3. A party always gives a problem a political colour, which turns it into a pretext. It tends to sow, in every economic, cultural or political project, the seeds of suspicion, whether in the intentions, purpose or objective. Such criticism is usually fabricated by the ruling regimes "in order to make the party look, in the eyes of public opinion, like one that harms the interests of the nation, which, in turn those regimes use to justify their dictatorships."[53] Criticism, however, does not invalidate the need for parties, nor does it prove that the party concept is a non-entity that has no justification in the turmoil of political life.

4. A party moulds its members into a particular ideological framework, i.e., it "renders necessary the narrowing of the mind of its members, so that right and wrong become immaterial to them,

---

[51] M. Shirazi, *al-Fiqh* series, volume 102, Politics, Article 38: p 138

[52] ibid., p 139

[53] ibid., p 145

what is important to party members is the view of the party, whatever that may be."[54] But is not this the case in every ideological, intellectual and political aspect, including sects, religion and beliefs? This applies even to language and homeland, let alone a party that is a product of the general structure of the society and its beliefs and needs; a party which melts into the society and embraces its spirit, without restrictions or narrowing of the minds.

5. Parties falsify democracy. This criticism may be re-directed against each and every political and organisational institution and body. A party that has confidence in its ideological programme and has a broad popular base need not play such games.

From all these observations we may conclude that Shirazi adopts and advocates the freedom of party activity yet within the context of a live vision, which respects mankind and his capability, and assigning an effective and vital role to human will. Within the framework of this vision Shirazi spots other effects relating to the essence and spirit of the idea.

I.   No ... to one party system
II.   No ... to dictatorial parties
III.   No ... to crude parties (that do not have clear political programmes)[55]

In conclusion, Shirazi presents his Islamic view of party political pluralism as follows:

- A party organisation becomes an assigned duty if and when it becomes a prelude to establishing an Islamic government.
- If other methods become available to establish Islamic rule, party activity becomes an optional duty.
- Party activity is prohibited if it turns out to be a prelude to creating a parliament that does not rule according to Islamic Law.
- Party activity is prohibited if it aims at running the political machine of the country without reference to and acting according to the jurisdiction of religious scholars.

---

[54] ibid.

[55] ibid.

- Party activity is prohibited if it turns out to be a cause for bringing to power someone not acceptable to the majority of the nation, even if that someone was a learned and a just religious scholar.
- A single party's monopoly of power is also prohibited, because Islam is a religion based and built on Shura... the consultative system.

This is Shirazi's general theory of party organisation. It has, built in it, all the elements of sound theoretical formation. Let us investigate this question in the light of the principle of scientific method.

A theoretical stance towards a phenomenon or a certain issue must stem from a clear basis that has a great respect and esteem in the mentality of definite rules; and has contents and implications that are neither ambiguous nor vague. A quick look at Shirazi's vision of party organisation will reveal the fact that it has all the necessary qualities and requirements. Yet, the progressive tendency is a forceful motive in Shirazi's vision of party organisation and activity. Openness, too, is the main quality of all these visions, all within the framework of the committed belief in man and his freedom.

The Social Revolution

Ayatollah Shirazi's writings on revolutions are very limited in volume, but the contents are abundant in meanings and vision. They seem to be the product of wide and deep readings into the revolutions of the world and the experiences of people and their historical struggles against tyrants.

Shirazi starts his discussion by defining revolution. He considers revolution as "social coup d' etat", i.e., and a tremendous transformation effecting, changing and substituting aspects of intellectual, political and economic life.[56] He thus gives the precise meaning of "revolution", vis-à-vis its other unsettled and loose meaning of no clear limits. [57] In this sense it is an action performed by the "majority of the people" [58], i.e., revolution is guided and calm action of the masses, not an impulsive or reactive act. Shirazi is of the opinion that a revolution is the climax of three principle provocations (material and moral persecution):

I.   Rejection of the ruling regime
II.   Despair of any reform
III.   Aim for a new social system [59]

As such, revolution is a kind of mutual dialogue between the masses, their aspiration and the ruling regime; that is, an interaction between a miserable present and an optimistic view of the future. A revolution is detonated only when such abject conditions deteriorate to an all-time low of social oppression, political pressure and intellectual terror.

In his "Mechanisms of Revolution" Shirazi explains his theory of revolution. He stresses that a revolution is none but the wider masses, which makes him totally different from Karl Marx, who sees revolution as industrial and proletariat. His clarity of vision contrasts sharply the confusion that Dubre's has become known for. Although the latter was a revolutionary activist, his theorisation was confused, for he looks at

---

[56] M. Shirazi, *al-Fiqh* series, volume110, Sociology: p 132

[57] Brenton, The Revolution, p 17

[58] M. Shirazi, *al-Fiqh* series, volume110, Sociology: p 132

[59] ibid.

revolution sometimes as the task of a vanguard of students and revolutionary intellectuals. On occasions, however, he views revolution as the task of a band of revolutionary adventurers who detonate the revolution by a bold military move. Dubre strikes a third note when he describes revolution as the task of the party raising the banner of the deprived.[60]

Shirazi differs on this issue with Herbert Marcus too, who believes that students are the spark of revolution, its energy, and its fuel, especially because the capitalist system has managed to dissipate the revolutionary spirit out of the working class.[61] Nor does Shirazi agree with Franz Vanon, who claims that ".. Peasants alone are the real revolutionaries in colonised countries, for they have nothing to lose, and the peasant, the starving and deprived -outside the class system - will be the first amongst the exploited, to discover that violence is the only useful means" [62]

It is masses that ignite the revolution, for injustice may befall every one, every body and every class. So, why shouldn't all the classes revolt? This is a fact that has been witnessed in many countries. In Shirazi's thought, a revolution is not "a jump in the air"; rather it is in stages. That is to say, its running on the ground escalates and accelerates in intensity and strength till it reaches the climax. The stages are:

1. Disturbance and discontent
2. Escalation of the social revolutionary spirit
3. Expansion of the revolution
4. Crystallising the one idea as an aim and a way
5. Finally, widening the ways effecting the realisation of the revolution.

1. In the state of disturbance and discontent, the result of the malpractices of the state, every individual may do whatever they deem fit, be it complaining, distributing secret leaflets, hints on platforms, or writing slogans on walls etc. The state may take some measures, though not very violent, against some of those, but once the individual uses violence, the state may respond with similar

---

[60] New views on Revolution, pp 181-182

[61] ibid., pp 283, 331

[62] ibid., p 37

29

violence, or even tougher measures, as deterrence that the state thinks and hopes would be decisive.

2. As the discontented gets closer together, and because the state's actions would bring about counter actions and reactions, the spirit of revolution gets inflamed. Despair fills the hearts, so much so that people begin to see that the only way out lies in them taking the necessary action. For here is a government, who would not listen to any complaint, rather than in any reform seeking satisfaction in the false promises they give and the threats they make, rather than in any reform...

3. As a result, the revolution expands and extends to other areas of the land and the society; people start to feel the need for a popular action, by the whole people. The action deemed necessary would not aim at reforming an aspect, or changing a minister, or eliciting fairness to a wronged individual; for, the problem is far greater than all this, and the state begins to deteriorate, from degradation to rude arrogance. It sees itself as the master of the field, which those opposing it are few gangsters whom the state, if so wished, could penetrate them and liquidate them with a heavy stick. And so the two opposing sides come to the point of confronting each other.

4. Only then would the revolutionary idea become crystallised, with the nation determined to overthrow the ruling regime, whatever the sacrifices. Small and modest leaderships begin to emerge and polarise, which attracts people's attention. They begin to see in those better alternatives than the state leadership.

5. Then comes the turn of the revolutionary establishment, thus widening the paths leading to the realisation of the revolution, which would bring chaos to the country. The government and the revolution establishment confront each other; the governments grip gets weaker, while that of the revolutionaries gets stronger.... The government tries a hand at compromises. The revolutionaries refuse. The government tries to avert its final downfall, offering some solutions, like changing some officials, cancelling some taxes, freeing some prisoners, or inviting some revolutionaries to share power with the government.

But it would then be too late, for the revolutionaries would quote: *"Now that you have disobeyed for too long, and were a corrupting agent"* [63]

The revolutionaries would now take charge of the state's establishments and institutions, one after the other. They would not be deterred by the half-hearted violence offered by the regime, like declaring a state of emergency, replacing the civilian government by a military one, imposing curfews, firing at demonstrators, looting strikers shops, etc.

Main figures of the government begin to flee or hide. Some of them are caught by the revolutionaries who would treat them cruelly, or leniently, depending on two things:

1. The extent of violence dealt to the revolutionaries by the government, for violence only produces violence.
2. The moral values of the revolution. Revolutionaries always adhere to ideal qualities; they compete and work hard to make themselves examples, which sometimes forces them to forego their legitimate rights.

Hence the savage revenge of the Bolshevik revolution against Tsar and his followers. The French revolution, however, was less revengeful.

As for the Islamic revolution, it was an expression of Allah, the compassionate, the merciful. The Prophet (PBUH) addressed his most vicious opponents when they fell in the grip of his Justice and probity, saying, *"Go! For you are now at liberty."*

Ali (PBUH) - appointed by the Prophet to succeed him after his death - conferred amnesty on the leaders of the muting during the Battle of the "Camel". Even 'Aisha, who spear headed the campaign, along with other leaders (of the rebel army) received his most generous treatment. He also forgave the leaders of the traitors at Nahrawan, and whenever he arrested any of the rebels of the battle of Siffin, he set him free on the condition that he would not support the enemy again.

Referring to this attitude, the poet says:

When we ruled, forgiveness was our Nature
And when you ruled, there were rivers of blood

---

[63] The holy Qur'an, Jonah (10): 91.

Your rule allows the Murder of the captives
But we forgave the captives and continued to free them

Suffice this difference between us
Through every container seeps its content

Ali (PBUH) says: *"If you rule, be forgiving'.*
He continues: *"Forgiveness is the alms of victory"...* [64]

Thus the most important consequence of a revolution lies in two (main) objectives:

A. Destroying the unjust regime[65]. For, a revolution ends once and for all the injustice of the bygone regime and begins a new era.

B. Distributing power or authority amongst groups, organisations and parties in such a way that no single organisation can monopolise rule and liquidate the others,[66] which means equality of opportunities, both in action and movement.

But Shirazi does not present this as a necessity, but as what the reality should be, and what the result will be like. Otherwise, take the French revolution, which ended up as a military colonialist dictatorship; and the Russian revolution, which has been turned into a rule of a tyrant minority.

If a revolution does not eliminate the very roots of a corrupt regime, and build a good regime or system, it will turn into a catastrophe inflicted on the people and the nation.

A desired outcome may be guaranteed if certain conditions are met: -

I.   An integral social programme
II.   A "clean" leadership

---

[64] *Nuhj-lu-Balgha* (Peak of Eloquence), p 506.
Nuhj-lu-Balgha is a collection of Sayings, Letters, and Speeches by Imam Ali (PBUH), appointed to be his successor by the prophet Muhammad (PBUH).

[65] M. Shirazi, *al-Fiqh* series, volume 133, Sociology: p 445

[66] ibid.

III.   Public awareness and vigilance

If a dictatorial authority usurps power, other consequences may follow, first and foremost of which is a counter-revolution, campaigns of terror and arrests, and, eventually, civil war.[67]

Creve Brenton details some of these consequences in his "Revolution: The Elements, Analysis and Results".

Ayatollah Shirazi believes in social revolution; and his deep belief in it emanates from its importance in the making of life and history. The only condition he lays is that a revolution must carry or bring with it the wind of change that will implant the bases and principles of freedom, justice and progress. That is why he rejects and refutes military *coup de tat* strongly and vehemently. He considers these as a form of piracy, for most of them, and for the last thirty or so years" have taken place as part of a colonialist, either Western or Eastern, plan or conspiracy".[68] The advocates of *coup d' etat* claim that "the regular-military action is a must, because the nation has lost its sense of direction or maturity, thus making military action the only means of change and, consequently, insisting that political power should remain in the hands of the military". This is one way of insulting the intelligence and the will of the nations, especially when we realise that the military's guardianship over the nation has been achieved only thanks to the arms and weaponry, which is not a rational justification for guardianship. Shirazi reminds us of the *coup d' etat* that have taken place, and asks us to look into the disasters they have brought with them, in the form of terror, suppression of freedoms etc.[69]

Ayatollah Shirazi reaches the climax of his theory of revolution when he reasserts the importance of its emanation from its social and historical milieus. In a loud voice he declares that " Every revolution must have its own roots". [70] By "roots" he means the nature, customs, traditions and ideas that constitute the history of a nation, what contemporary writers call "the free conscience of a nation". Today, this formula is a great

---

[67] ibid.

[68] ibid., pp 452-454

[69] ibid.

[70] ibid.

theory of human thought, which deals with revolution, construction and change. The last thirty years or so of this century are called the era of "returning to roots". Yet Shirazi is not oblivious of the role external factors play in the process of change, be it backing or support offered by states, people or institutions.[71]

These are the outlines of the theory of revolution in the political thought advocated and initiated by Ayatollah Shirazi. They may be summed up in the following points:

- The definition: "A Revolution is a fundamental social coup".
- The tools: "The wider masses".
- The causes: "Total social oppression combined with frustration with the status quo"
- The desired result: "destruction of the unjust regime, and building a new society based on freedom, Justice and progress".
- The basic condition: "Emanation from the roots".
- The basic requirement: "A clean programme, revolutionary ethics, and honest leaderships".
- The stages: "Disturbance and discontent; escalation of the rejectionist spirit, expansion of rejection, Crystallising of ideas and revolutionary wills; availability of several methods to strike against the opponent (the ruling regime); the final result
- The outcome: "A new social and political life abundant with hope, optimism and giving, but only if the masses are well aware of the role they have to play, and if they do not allow a small faction to steal the revolution and liquidate others. Otherwise, a tyrant dictatorship might ensue, if the masses fail to play their part, and fail to safeguard, through their awareness, vigilance and clear stances, the gains of the revolution.

---

[71] ibid.

Non-Violence

Non-violence, or peace, is an essential pillar of the political theory presented and advocated by Ayatollah Shirazi in all his books, researches and studies.

Peace is:
- An aim and objective, on the one hand,
- And, on the other, a means and a way.

That is to say, peace is a total strategic principle.[72] Within this framework, Shirazi puts forward the following slogans: -

- Peace always and forever [73]
- Peace is the guarantee for the maintenance of a principle[74]
- Peace produces the safest and best consequences [75]
- Peace in speeches, peace in the writings, peace in action, and peace everywhere and with everyone.[76]

In this very wide sense of the word, peace does not become an obsession, as some like to think; rather, it is a total political vision. First because of its totality and the assertion it enjoys as a quality.

An obsession is a sudden, temporary interjection, whereas a vision is steadiness, continuity, insight and guidance.

Ayatollah Shirazi builds this total and comprehensive vision of peace, remarkable as it surely is, relying on an important collection of justifications and reasoning. Of these are:

1- The Islamic Legal evidence

---

[72] M. Shirazi, The Way to Muslim Revival, p 199

[73] ibid., p 201

[74] ibid., p 209

[75] ibid., p 196

[76] ibid., p 198

There are a great number of these in the Qur'an and the Teaching of the Prophet (Sunnah). The texts call for peace as a slogan, a starting point, an aim and objective, and a course of action.

Allah the Almighty states in the Qur'an:

"Do enter all in peace, and do not follow the steps of Satan",

"And their greetings in it (paradise) is peace",

"Be kind and courteous, and you will soon find that those with whom you have enmity become very close friends... Only those who show patience (perseverance) will enjoy this; only those with great luck shall do".

"Do not swear at those who seek (Deity) in other than God",

The prophet is quoted as saying,

"O Ali, the best of qualities in this life and the hereafter are words of courtesy, generosity, and to forgive those who inflict injustice on you".

. . . and many other Teachings to this effect.

2- The Infallible Tradition

When Makkah fell, the Prophet pardoned the (tribe of) Quraysh, including the most vicious of that tribe, who persecuted him, expelled him and fought battles against him. To them he said the well-known phrase:

"Go! For you are now at liberty."

Ali (PBUH) never fought his enemies in the battles of "the Camel", "Nahrawan" and "Siffin", without first giving them the unequivocal answers to their arguments, and gave them warnings and plenty of opportunities to reflect. Even when he won his victory over them, he never took revenge on any of them. He pardoned them all. Imam Hussain (PBUH) did the same. Imam Ali's slogan after the fall of Makkah was: *Today is the day of mercy; today, the inviolables are protected.*

3- Sound Thought

For it leads to peace, and saves lives, brings plenty to all, protects the honour and chastity of human beings, expands human relations, and enables the good earth to give its best.

4- Experience

For all the governments, regimes and parties that used violence have vanished, or are on their way to demise. Peoples and nations in particular and mankind in general hate them.

Peace according to Ayatollah Shirazi, is the anti-thesis of:

1. War. For war is the worst thing mankind has ever known. Wars are a direct cause of the destruction of man in every respect; socially, psychologically and from the civilisation viewpoint. Wars are total destruction [77]. This is a right and a wise judgement, and there is no doubt that "all civilisations of the past have been destroyed by wars." [78]. Suffice it to say that wars "are the inevitable encounter with death, be it by accident or by fighting."[79]

2. Violence. For, violence is an abnormality that paralyses man's movement, and blocks the psychological channels between people and rulers and the regimes, which practice violence openly and secretly. Violence is a state of behaviour that totally controls the violent; for, "the violent person is equally so with both friends and strangers, with aliens as well as with enemies". [80] It is a (second) nature, yet an abnormal one.

Shirazi rejects all forms of violence...

---

[77] M. Shirazi, "The New Order for the World of Faith, Freedom, Prosperity and Peace", p349.

[78] Wars and Civilisation, p36.

[79] ibid., p28.

[80] M. Shirazi, "The Way to Muslim Revival", p 191.

- Be it straightforward violence, as when a man forces another to sign a pledge, under the threat of murder [81]. Force and coercion are illegal in Islam.

- Or less visible violence, as when an employer forces an employee to do a job, exploiting a psychological or livelihood weakness in him.[82] This is similar to exploitation or blackmail.

- Or silent violence: whereby a bureaucratic system exhausts the patience of citizens who eventually succumb to it. [83] Bureaucracy is the disease of civilisation.

Peace, therefore, is a project, an idea, a theory, and a vision... In contrast, war is coercion and dictatorship, which are of close and similar qualities. That is why we have stated that peace is a framework in the political thought of Ayatollah Shirazi.

Yet he speaks in detail of peace in the field of the Islamic movement. He thus puts forward the following criteria:

1. The Islamic movement must adopt peace as a slogan, for it is the symbol and motto of Islam, peace of the world, of the country, of the family, and peace of the whole society.

2. Relations between members of the movement must be based on peace. " Members must have complete harmony, and there should not be disputes and disagreements between them..." [84]

3. The relation between the movement and others based on this honourable human principle, i.e. peace. To that effect he says, "The activists of the movement must embody peace in their thought, words and actions, towards both friends and foes" [85]

---

[81] Psychology of politics, pp 182-200. Also note Shirazi's view on this topic in "Politics", "Sociology", "Government in Islam" and "The New Order for the World of Faith, Freedom, Prosperity and Peace"

[82] ibid.

[83] ibid.

[84] M. Shirazi, "The Way to Muslim Revival", p 208

[85] ibid., p 190

4. The movement must do its utmost to educate its members to the tune of this great moral value. "The movement must educate its cadres according to the ethics of peace in words, thought, writing, and deeds, whatever the cost" [86], he says.

5. Peace should be the Islamic movement's means to achieve its objectives, for "war, boycott and other methods of violence, as well as abnormal emergencies are, unlike the Islamic fundamental principles, similar to eating a dead animal's carcass out of desperate necessity..." [87]

Achieving peace within the Islamic movement is possible if two conditions are met: [88]

A. If free elections are held
B. If consultation (Shura) is practised within the movement.

Peace with other movements can be achieved by adopting a policy of tolerance, exchange of ideas, intellectual dialogue and free scientific and objective debates.[89]

Peace for all movement, therefore, is an objective, a programme and a system.
For the Islamic state, however, peace is a far greater task: It is that state's message to the world and its international target, which it tries to reach. To that effect Shirazi says, "The Islamic State must advocate peace:

(O you who have believed, enter all in peace) [90]

And move towards peace in response to a similar attitude by non-Islamic state:

If they move towards peace, move towards them, too.[91]

---

[86] ibid., p 202

[87] ibid., p 183

[88] ibid., pp 223-225

[89] ibid.

[90] The holy Qur'an, Cow (2): 208.

If the Islamic state is forced to wage an external war or to quell an internal disturbance, it must do so according to the most ideal and humanitarian principle. For, war is very much like a surgical operation, only implemented when absolutely necessary..."[92] This is the idea in general. Yet, Shirazi gives further details on the responsibility of the Islamic State towards world peace. He believes that the Muslim State should work for peace through:

I.   Stopping the arms race,
II.   Containing the idea of military coups,
III.   Giving the role of the United Nations real effectiveness by invalidating the right of veto,
IV.   Spreading social justice throughout the world,
V.   Calling for human virtues. [93]

We can easily see a dialectical relationship, in the theory of Shirazi, between world peace and world social justice. This is a point of view strongly advocated by contemporary studies. Lister Pearson, a Nobel Prize winner, is one such example. "Welfare of peoples is one of the pillars of peace;" he writes, "this issue has witnessed a great interest and development in our minds recently." [94]

There is no doubt that there is an inherent relationship between peace and the containment of the formidable arms race, which threatens the whole world. There is a spiritual and creative interrelationship between peace and morals. According to Spinoza, "Peace is none but the determination that emanates from the virtues of the soul." [95]

Thus, the theoretical construction of the world peace is completed in and through the policies of the Islamic State. Peace is a relentless effort, with which emotions, intellect, material, spirit and will interact.

---

[91] The holy Qur'an, Public Estates (8): 61.

[92] ibid.

[93] ibid.

[94] L. Pearson, "Diplomacy in the Nuclear era", p 93

[95] ibid., p106

Political action to establish the Islamic government must be based on peace. Shirazi rejects violence as a means to achieve the great ideological objective.

After a long discussion of the life and the Teachings of the messenger of Allah, he adds:

"...The Islamic movement starts by attracting followers, organising itself, and seeking awareness. It then overthrows, directly, the colonialist regimes, and the satellite regimes, either by strikes, demonstrations and if it was compelled to war, it should not initiate the war, so it has the stronger argument against the aggressor before the world. If it could, it should avert war by peaceful means. Only if peaceful means fail does it allocate "one fourth" of its activities to war, and three quarters to peaceful solutions.[96]

But he says "No" to violence. Why?

1. Because killing will entail retaliation, in all societies and nations. They say that Islam is the religion of killing. People view the action of rulers ruling in the name of a certain doctrine as a "practical experiment" of that doctrine, that is why they consider Nazism, Fascism and communism as ideologies of murderers like Hitler, Mussolini and Stalin. When peoples to such ideologies expressed a reaction, they would no doubt conspire to overthrow such regimes. Peoples' schemes do produce results in their downfall and the fall and demise of their ideologies?[97]

2. Because killing entails the turn of the nation against the ruling regime. The nation might be weak. But the scales can be tipped in favour of the nation and, consequently, against that ideology or that state. Then the eventual fall, or even the total liquidation, comes, as we saw in the case of the Umayyad dynasty, which were liquidated by the nation; and as in the case of others who took killing as a profession.[98]

---

[96]M. Shirazi, *al-Fiqh* series, Volumes 109-110, "Politics"

[97] ibid.

[98] ibid.

It is necessary, therefore, for the Islamic trend, before establishing a state, i.e., the Muslim State, to avert war in every possible way. For killing provokes people beyond description. People never forget those who kill their sons, relatives and friends.

Even if such actions did not leave any immediate impact during the era of the prevailing strengths of a certain ideology or state, they would be bound to make their inevitable impact on the long run.[99]

---

[99] ibid.

Justice

In Islam, justice is a great, wide and important issue, because it relates to far reaching aspects of that faith:

- **Doctrine**: God's justice is one of the pillars of the Islamic faith.
- **Existence**: Justice in a cosmic sense is inherent in the Islamic vision of the universe, where existence (of the universe) is balanced and coherent: *We have grown everything in balance.* [100]
- **Conduct**: Islam requires every Muslim to conduct all her/his behaviour in a just manner i.e. a committed Muslim. This conduct is also the pre-condition that a ruler, religious scholar and even a prayer leader must have.
- **Social**: Justice as a social need is also an Islamic principle, which means that the society and its motion must be founded on a balanced basis, in rights and duties, irrespective of any marginal consideration, be it colour race or language.

Some of Shirazi's statements on justice in the behavioural and social domains are characterised by a didactic, almost emotional tone, while other statements have the vigour of ideology and theorisation.

On the issue of preparing the human conscience, and loading the human spirit with the instinct of justice, Ayatollah Shirazi gives, as examples, a number of real - life stories in a small booklet called "Justice: the basis of government". Beautifully written, it provides food for thought and lessons to be learned on the value of justice in this life.

Theoretically, Shirazi is of the opinion that:

1- The Foundation of the Islamic State.

Justice is one of the pillars on which the Islamic State stands, and it involves all aspects of life, even "with enemies; and even in small matters". [101] Shirazi draws his evidence from the Qur'an and the Teachings of the prophet stipulating "the obligatory nature of justice".

---

[100] The holy Qur'an, *Hijr* City (15): 19

[101] M. Shirazi, "The New order for the World of Faith, Freedom, Prosperity and Peace"

43

2- Equal Opportunity

Economic justice means bringing classes closer together rather than striking total equality amongst them. This cannot be achieved through automatic distribution of wealth, as some people imagine, for such is a backward and primitive method. Justice can be achieved, however, through equal opportunities provided to all people.

In his book "Economics" (Case no. 9), Shirazi says, "it is necessary to guarantee all people equality in economic matters, for all people are the offspring of one father and one mother..."[102]

3- Ownership

In this respect, Shirazi rejects the two extreme forms of ownership, i.e. the capitalist and the Marxist forms of ownership. Human economics tend to admit and recognise moderate ownership, now that both experiments, the Western and the Eastern, have failed in this respect.[103]

4- Redistribution of Wealth

Under this heading comes the principle of equality of giving stipulated and reasserted by Ali following his succession to the government. In stipulating this principle, Shirazi draws further evidence of this economic factor included in his concept of justice from a number of Islamic legal texts, as well as from the traditions of Ali (PBUH). [104]

Allah states:
"... Whatever God had conferred on his messenger (from gains taken) from people of the cities, (goes) to God, the messenger, the kinsmen, the orphans and the travellers, so that it may not circulate amongst the rich amongst you. What the messenger gives you, take it; and what he forbids you to take, don't. Fear God, for God's punishment is verily great"[105].

---

[102] M. Shirazi, al-Fiqh series, volumes 107-108, "Economics"

[103] ibid., p 184-193.

[104] M. Shirazi, "New Order for the World of Faith, Freedom, Prosperity and Peace"

[105] The holy Qur'an: Banishment (59): 7

The sixth Imam, Sadiq, is quoted as saying, *"He who takes charge of one aspect of peoples' affairs, and deals with them justly, and is available for people to solve their problems, Allah verily guarantees his security on the day of Judgement and admits him to paradise.*

He is also quoted as saying, *"The people of Islam are the children of Islam: I treat them all as equal when I give. As for their virtues, it is a matter between them and Allah. I treat them as if they were the children of one man; none of them is given priority on grounds of his virtue or piety..."*

5- Criteria for the Ruler

Finally, justice is a quality, which a religious scholar must possess in order to satisfy one of the criteria of being religious authority and/or leader. This will be later discussed under "Council of religious authority".

A quick look at this set of elements and conditions would easily reveal that justice according to Ayatollah Shirazi is a social value as much as a philosophical one. It is second nature in intellectuals who put man on top of their intellectual concerns to speak of justice in its objective sense more than as a metaphysical concept.

Shirazi bonds justice and good deeds together, hence his comments on some Qur'anic Verses ordaining justice and probity, "...He who exercises justice in all cases is the one who has done good deeds."[106] Justice, according to Ayatollah Shirazi, is a creative power, reviving right and destroying injustice. G. Lewis Dickinson, the well-known philosopher and politician, arrives at similar conclusion when he states that, "justice is a power, and if that power cannot create something, it can, at least, inflict destruction..." [107]

Justice in this broad sense, according to Shirazi, is one of the main objectives of the Islamic State.

---

[106] M. Shirazi, "New Order for the World of Faith, Freedom, Prosperity and Peace"

[107] Harold Laskie, "Government - Theory and Practice", vol. 2, p 7

Under "Case No. 29" he states that, "Of the main issues, which concern the Islamic State, is justice and kindness, which is above justice). If you gave an employee his dues, this would be justice. If you gave him more, that would be kindness." [108]

Yet, Shirazi deepens the relation between justice and kindness; he sees the latter as a sublimation of the former and its perfection, lifting justice even higher. But how?

He states: "Justice in terms of the law is what Islam terms kindness which is closer to reality. In any case, there are "equality", "justice", and "kindness". Allah says, *"Allah has ordained justice, and kindness".[109]*
Equality could be just or it may not be so, and vice versa. For example, if inheritance is divided equally between two brothers, this is equality and justice, but if an older brother and younger one were given the same length of cloth to make clothes for themselves this would be equality but not justice. If they were each given according to his needs that would be justice but not equality.

Justice means giving every one their right dues, and holding every wrong doer responsible for their own wrongdoing. Kindness, on the other hand, means giving one more than what one is rightly entitled to, provided that this does not harm or eat into the right of others. Pardoning a criminal, for example, is kindness, provided that it does not invalidate or annul another right. Kindness is higher up the law; for the law stipulates rights, duties and indictments only, whereas kindness is an effort to make life easier; the climate, cooler. The state should take this into consideration, so that the law may turn into a lush oasis, abundant with mercy and compassion for man. Kindness aims at strengthening the ties between the state and the nation, and guiding that nation forward. The mutual relation between the two necessitates a certain degree of trust, freedom and welfare. All of these are essentials for progress, even for security, tranquillity and relief from unease." [110]

---

[108] M. Shirazi, *al-Fiqh* series, "Government in Islam", p 157

[109] The Qur'an, The Bee (16): 90

[110] M. Shirazi, *al-Fiqh* series, vol. 106 Politics, p 290-291

Islamic Unity

According to Shirazi's political vision, Islamic unity consists of the following aspects: -

1. The idea
2. Aspects and fields
3. Methods and Tools

Accordingly, the issue of "The Islamic Unity" forms a project that is a component of the political vision adopted by Ayatollah Shirazi.

The Idea

The idea of "Islamic Unity" stems from a number of basic, indisputable, Islamic principles. The Islamic faiths as well as the history and common destiny are examples of the principles, which unite the Muslims.
All the Muslims are united on many aspects of those principles. They are therefore bound to unite. Islamic unity is a necessity emanating from "Islamic brotherhood" [111] as stipulated in the Qur'an: *"All believers are verily brothers"*. The same emanates from the concept of "the Muslim Ommah or Community" [112], which is one nation according to the Qur'an. *"... This is your Community, one and united; I am your Lord, and Me you shall worship..."*

Thus the idea of Islamic unity is a natural outcome of all these precepts that are taken for granted and are a matter of Islamic fact. On this the majority of Muslim scholars, both Shi'a and Sunni, agree.

Aspects and Fields

Unity as an idea is proposed in current debates, but only as an abstract, a concept, and in terms of a rosy wish and a slogan.

---

[111] M. Shirazi, "The New order for the World of Faith, Freedom, Prosperity and Peace", p 491

[112] ibid., p 487

The majority of those who advocate unity imply "sectarian unity" i.e. the unity of Shi'a and Sunni. This is where the weakness of most of those calls lies, as they emanate from an oversimplified meaning of "unity" and from a simplified understanding.

Unity in the sense of co-operation, mutual support and understanding is a huge and vast project and for both Shi'a and Sunni it may be at its last stages. From this responsible vision Shirazi moves to the crucial debate on Islamic unity.

It is a proposal, which has emanated from a real and affectionate experience in the Islamic field in the Islamic cause in all its aspects and vast areas of active initiatives. That is why he discusses the issue in more than one aspect and on more than one occasion: -

I.   Unity of the Islamic Leadership

This is embodied in the "Council of Religious Authorities" - a consultative system of leadership as presented by Shirazi when dealing with the administration of the Islamic State. This is the very idea, which he aims to turn into reality now, with all his power and using all the intellectual energy he can muster. And he enjoys the support of many Muslim activists. This issue is discussed in another chapter of this book.

II.   Unity of the Islamic Movement

This issue occupies a vast area of Shirazi's invaluable studies, published in his "Towards Muslim Revival". According to this study, the foundation and basis of this unity is "the iron organisation, for, if an organisation is loose, and if the grassroots differs with the leadership, the whole system will end up in failure" [113]. He believes that there are three bases, which guarantee this unity, in addition of course, to the unity of ideology and objective. The three bases are: -

A. Commitment and respect to the leadership by the bases
B. The election of the leadership by the members of the organisation. Since if there were no free elections of the leadership by the bases, the interaction between the two would not be honest, or based on conviction.

---

[113] M. Shirazi, "The Way to Muslim Revival", p 79.

C. Disciplinary measures against those flouting the rules. [114]

The party, the organisation or the movement must have, as an essential concept, the element and principle of strict internal unity in order to play its vital role.

III.   Unity of the Islamic Movements

Shirazi believes in the impending necessity of the "One world Islamic Movement". This is the core of his political thought. To that effect he says,
"There is one movement in Iran, another in Iraq, a third in the Gulf and other movements in India, Pakistan, North Africa, Egypt and Sudan. There are movements in the Americas, Europe, Japan, China and the Soviet Union. It is necessary for all those movements to unite in one single movement as long as the objective is one, and the issue is the same. All of them complain of colonialism, exploitation, dictatorship and civilisation backwardness etc."[115]

The unity of the Islamic movement, all its organisations, parties etc. has become an impending necessity, now that the enemies have taken the unequivocal decision to confront Islam in a war of life or death. Strength will come only from unity; if all the Islamic movements were united, they would become a formidable force capable of confronting foreign colonialism and internal backwardness." [116]

Shirazi does not ignore the role of Islamic legislation (*Ijtihad*) in this respect. He admits the possibility of divergence of opinion on this issue amongst the Islamic movements, yet he does not consider that as a real obstacle. "Divergence of Islamic legislation would not harm the issue of unity", he writes, "for differing is a natural thing in human beings. Activists - however sincere - are bound to make different decisions (*Ijtihad*)." To solve this problem, Shirazi suggests "implementing the views of the majority" [117], but according to Islamic criteria. Such unity, he adds, requires two aspects: -

---

[114] ibid., pp77-78

[115] ibid., p 65

[116] ibid., p 66

[117] ibid.

A. "to ignore shortcomings and to forgive mistakes; to forget disputes and quarrels"

B. "to have joint actions, as, for example, when the general leadership of all those movements decide to declare a general strike on a certain day, from Tangiers in the West to Djakarta in the East, and from Kabul to the farthest West" [118]

Such joint actions must, of course, be preceded by a unity of method, political thought, struggle and organisational approaches, even in a general sense.

IV.   *Unity of Muslims (Sunni and Shi'a)*

Shirazi discusses this issue by addressing the most important and at the same time the most difficult aspect of this topic, which is the subject of the united government for all the Muslims. This topic has not been addressed and discussed as thorough as necessary. This is a remarkable idea, and a penetration into the far depths of the complications and implications of the issue, especially if we take into consideration the fact that unity in the sense of total sectarian fusion is alien to reality and logic. Even meeting on common grounds is a much-argued issue. Yet this unity, with the issue of the ruling regime complex in mind, in what lacks interest, discussion and treatment. By tackling the subject from this angle, Shirazi is taking an ideological and political risk, or even gamble, for the consequences and after- effects will not escape criticism. The risk is nonetheless; based on solid grounds because it is wrought with thought and (creative) imagination.

To this effect Shirazi says, `There are a thousand million Muslims in this world, almost half of whom are Shi'a and the other half Sunni. They share joint life in all the countries and, in some countries the Shi'a are the majority; in others the Sunni, and in some other countries they are of equal numbers. If we wanted to bring those Sunni and Shi'a together in a religious and ideological unity, we should fulfil a number of conditions:

1. We should bring all Shi'a religious authorities together in one Supreme Council that take decision by majority vote.

---

[118] ibid., p 69

2. We should bring all Sunnis religious authorities and scholars following them together in a Supreme Council that takes decision by the majority vote...

3. Those two Supreme Councils should be combined together in one council. If a ruling were to be made concerning one sect (school of thought) only, the scholars of that sect can make such ruling by majority of vote (of their respective Supreme council). If the ruling effects all Muslims, i.e.' all the one thousand million Muslims on matters of peace and war etc., the ruling should be taken by majority of vote of both councils, yet the majority in one Council should never mean that it is the absolute majority.

4. Each one of the two sects has the full right and freedom to discuss fundamental and minor issues; but neither sect has any right to attack the other physically.

5. From the Supreme council and the scholars assembly (consultative bodies) will emerge free Islamic parties, each in their respective sectarian milieu. Those parties should become schools of economic, social and educational thought aimed at preparing the suitable cadre to administer the country in all legislative, judicial and executive sectors.

6. Rulers should be chosen from the majority in any one country, provided that such an arrangement does not restrict or limit the freedom of the minority. The same applies to the judiciary and the like.

7. The duty of all those scholars and parties must be to bring this one Community back to life, and to refer the ultimate leadership and judgement back to Allah the almighty. [119]

A look into this proposition would no doubt reveal its realistic approach and respect for the others. It has the practical formula, which translates sectarian agreement into real tangible action.

As mentioned before, Shirazi tends here to break the political and social taboos in a bold and courageous manner. For the issue of Islamic unity in the field of leadership is the most crucial and complex aspect. The

---

[119]M. Shirazi, "How to Unite the Muslims"

bloodshed inflicted in Shi'a and Sunni may be due to a number of reasons, most important and serious of which being leadership.

Ayatollah Shirazi does not believe in rosy words as means to achieve an objective, let alone an objective such as "Islamic unity". Rather, it is the practice based on a clear and practical proposition, is the only way to achieving that.

It must be mentioned, however, that in submitting this vital proposition, Shirazi's school of thought has drawn on all the elements of entity, effect and influence on both sects, the Sunni and Shi'a. He has put forward his unitary visions only after combining all these elements in his mind and thought.

In his theoretical introduction he states that, "It is easy to raise Islamic unity as a slogan and an alternative to emotions emanating from the heart. To give it its mantle of direct realisation, however, needs a wholly integrated vision and proposition, covering, on the one hand, the Community and the state, and, on the other, all the traditional trends, religious authorities and scholars."[120]

V.   Unity of the Shi'a Entity

According to Shirazi, this entity is composed of three main elements:

1.   The supreme religious authority and other religious authorities,
2.   Regional scholars, scholars of religious Shi'a schools, and all those who belong to this circle,
3.   The Community.

Methods and Tools

Shirazi is of the opinion that the unity of this entity can be achieved if every one of these three elements performs its duties as required. Only then would ideas, thoughts and objectives be united.

What are the duties of a Religious Authority? They are, in short:

---

[120] ibid.

(a) To answer questions
(b) To give fatwa (religious ruling)
(c) To guide people
(d) To call for Islam
(e) To order virtuous deeds
(f) To forbid vile deeds
(g) To write and publish books treatise, papers, etc.
(h) To organise religious schools
(i) To send agents
(j) To effect reconciliation and reform
(k) To send missionaries
(l) To collect and distribute money
(m) To raise the standard of Muslims
(n) To be a judge
(o) To deter the unjust from inflicting harm on those wronged
(p) To protect the laws of Islam and uphold them
(q) To prevent void ideas from infiltrating (the Muslim State)
(r) To give the unjustly treated their dues (to deter and prevent injustice)
(s) To meet people's needs
(t) To protect the land of Islam against the enemies. [121]

The second and consequent question is what are the duties of scholars? In a word they are:

a) Educating and teaching
b) Teaching moral values
c) Making speeches
d) Writing books
e) Running educational institutions
f) Acting as agents (deputies) for Religious Authority
g) Calling for Islam
h) Giving advice to Religious Authority. [122]

It is quite clear that the main requirement for all those duties is specialised scholarship. Yet this does not mean overlapping, especially when the chances of movement and formation are scanty, and the security and political conditions are difficult.

---

[121] M. Shirazi, "The Religious Authority and the People", pp 11-13

[122] ibid., pp 39-40

The third question is "What are the duties of the community?" They are:

(a) To follow Religious Authority when making a legal Islamic ruling (judgement)
(b) To obey Religious Authority
(c) To give them their dues
(d) To support them in all matters
(e) To unite behind them
(f) To seek their advice in matters of judicial nature
(g) To ask them for agents (deputies)
(h) To keep them informed of what happens in the society
(i) To defend them
(j) To prepare and create the right circumstances for them
(k) To do their duties towards improving life (conditions) and building civilisation.[123]

---

[123] ibid.

The System of Consultation (Shura)

Council of Religious Authorities

Ayatollah Shirazi's vision of leadership in Islam is in line with his bold and courageous views on freedom, justice and revolution. Moreover, this vision is based on evidence from the Qur'an and the teachings of the prophet. The essence of this vision lies, as is well known, in the (leadership) Council of Religious Authorities.

Yet this system of leadership is neither a mere political slogan nor a propaganda poster. Rather, it is an Islamic view on this subject based on proof and evidence from the Qur'an and the Teaching of the prophet. It addresses the issue of leadership in Islam in great detail.

Anyone well read in the legacy of Shirazi will find that he shows great and effective interest in the "Council". He refers to it from time to time, and it seems that his aversion to dictatorship and his deep love for mankind and Islam combine to create a very important psychological reality and motive in this respect.

Ayatollah Shirazi has published some outstanding works dealing with this issue. Under the title, "Government in Islam", volume 99 of his *Fiqh* series, he delves in what amounts to an expanded, detailed evidential jurisprudence. In this work, he describes his theory of leadership in Islam in 34 case studies. He discusses them in full detail, as he does in his other and equally voluminous works such as "Politics", and "Sociology"; volumes 105-106 and 109-110 of the *Fiqh* series respectively, "Thus is the Rule of Islam", "Towards Muslim Revival", "Universal Islamic Government" and in many other works. This *Fiqh* series is one of the most remarkable works on *Fiqh* (Islamic legislation) ever published. This works covers various aspects such as Government, Politics, Economics, Sociology, Freedoms, Rights, Law, Judiciary, Contract, Marriage, etc. The *Fiqh* series constitutes 150 volumes, which run into more than 55,000 pages.

Islamic Legislative

Legislative Authority of the Messenger and Imams

Shirazi explains his theory of leadership, starting with the question of legislative authority. He asserts without any doubt that it is the right of the Prophet and the Imams[124], but not in a sense that "they are the law or its makers"[125], for that is the right of Allah the Almighty alone. Rather, they explain this legislation for people. Shirazi actually draws the evidence of the total and exclusive divine entitlement to legislation from the Qur'anic Verse *"Rule is the privilege of Allah (alone)"*.

On the role of prophets and imams as interpreters of the law of Allah, he draws evidence from the Qur'anic Verse *"do remind, for you are none but a reminder"*. And from the Qur'anic verse:
"And if he fabricates words he attributes (falsely) to us, we would demand his oath, and then inflict the heaviest punishment on him".

He quotes many other Verses, then lists support from teachings of the prophet and consensus of the scholars, then concludes as follows: -

" In any case, ... authority is, first and foremost, Allah's then the Messenger's and then the Imam's. Each of them has the privilege of universal authority, and the authority of legislation; yet Allah's authority is innate, personal, and subjective. As for his representatives, it is rather drawing on Him, His permission. Legislation as applied to them means only their right to explain the law of Allah the Almighty, not doctrinal legislation parallel to the authority of Allah" [126]

On this basis, we can conclude that the legislative authority, as a temporary authority, is a confirmed privilege of the Messenger and the Imams.

---

[124] They are those appointed by the Prophet to succeed him to lead the Muslims.

[125] M. Shirazi, *al-Fiqh* series vol. 99, "Government in Islam", p11

[126] ibid., p 17

Transition of the Authority to Religious Scholars

In the absence of the infallible imam should the Islamic law be suspended?

In his gradual exposition of his theory of leadership in Islam, Shirazi states that the General Legislative Authority of the prophets and the Imams is transferred to the religious scholar who meets the criteria. (Such scholar is referred to as Religious Authority.)

He draws evidence from the Qur'an, the Sunnah, consensus and reason to the effect that the religious scholar who meets the conditions and requirements enjoys the General Legislative Authority. He supports the consensus view that "a large number of scholars used to administer and deal with the affairs of the state and general politics", and relates evidence to the effect that the community had certain commitments towards religious scholars, and its loyalty and allegiance to them on various issues. [127]

How Do the Religious Scholars Come to Power?

Ayatollah Shirazi does not confine his scope to this limit, but goes further into clear and programmed detail on how do religious scholars come to power? This is a very serious, important and essential question. The Prophet became ruler through call to Islam, by gathering supporters, by engaging defensive war, in defence of the faith and life. The interaction between these calamities led him to rule Madinah. It was the Messenger that, on the orders of the Almighty, appointed the twelve infallible Imams to succeed him to lead the community. What is the way in which the religious scholars assume this honourable decoration?

Here, Shirazi strongly defends the idea of elections. It is the community that chooses its leader, according to the political Islamic theory of Shirazi.

He says, "The Muslim ruler is he who fulfils two conditions: -

1.   That he pleases Allah the Almighty

---

[127] ibid., p 26

2.   That he is elected by the majority of the community.[128]

In order to further clarify the idea, Shirazi says, "Government in Islam is neither bad or dictatorial. A ruler who comes to power through a military coup is totally unacceptable to Islam even if the ruler were a Muslim; for Islam demands that the opinion of the majority be the one adopted". Such election should never be "ceremonial", i.e., loaded with demonstration and rallies. It is also "necessary to hold periodic general elections to elect the head of state and the regional governors, also according to the vote of the majority."[129]

Method of Election

Ayatollah Shirazi discusses the issue of leadership in further detail so that the complete picture of the landmarks of a comprehensive school is clear.

How are the elections held?

The question has got to be addressed, since demonstrations and rallies supporting a certain candidate may be used as a proof that the candidate is or elected. Shirazi rejects this approach, as previously stated, and advocates elections in their familiar legal and political sense. But how?

His answer is, "The nation has the right to appoint the head of state through voting or elect a group of those to appoint the head of state. Thus the delusion is refuted, namely that "elections are unknown to the Islamic method, so how can Muslims advocate them?" [130]

On the basis of this viewpoint we come to the conclusion that election may be direct or indirect. Direct elections are those held by the nation in order to choose its leader without an intermediary. Indirect elections are those that are administered by representative elected by the nation.

---

[128] M. Shirazi, al-Fiqh series, volume 101, "Politics", p 504

[129] M. Shirazi, " The Way to Muslim Revival "

[130] M. Shirazi, al-Fiqh series, vol. 99, "Government in Islam", p41

Both methods embody the will of the Muslim nation in choosing its leader. Opting for one or the other depends on the circumstances and the atmosphere.

The Final Picture

Later, Shirazi details the final picture of the conditions likely to be the consequence of the election process. It is clarified as follows:

1. That the people choose a qualified religious authority (*Faqih*) "to be the one who takes charge of all matters. This is called "*Wilayat Faqih*" (the leadership of the religious authority).

2. Alternatively, the people choose a number of religious authorities (*Faqih's*) to be the collective head of the state on the basis of *Council of Religious Authority*. In the case of Council of Religious Authority, a new solution emerges; the situation is bound to be one of the two:

I.   Either the elected Faqihs select one of them as the leader, while the rest form the consultative body advising him, thus becoming "advisors",

II.   Or the concept of "collective leadership" is put into effect, whereby the affairs of the state and leadership are executed (by the whole body of elected jurists)[131]

In accordance with the above, "...The head of the Islamic state is the Faqih (jurist) who meets the set criteria, be it an individual or a collective body, according to the community's will and choice".

It is quite clear that if the Community will choose more than one Faqih who fulfil the conditions of leadership, which results in a governing and ruling body, the nation will then have opted for the "council of religious authorities" as a practical form of Islamic rule.

This leads to a serious result, namely that "council of religious authorities" as a method of rule, is subject to the community's approval. In this way Shirazi reaches the top of being honest to one's self on the

---

[131]M. Shirazi, *al-Fiqh* series, volume 101, "Politics", p 505

intellectual and ideological level... For, although he finds in "council of religious authorities" the most exemplary, accurate, remarkable and capable form of state administration, he insists that such form should never be imposed on the nation by force, ambiguity, or any other method of imposition. It should be the outcome of total public elections, whereby the election process plays a positive and effective role. We thus fall back on the first principle established by Ayatollah Shirazi, i.e., the need to appoint a ruler, whether a single individual or a collective body, through elections.

An Initial Conclusion

If we wished to draw a consequential gradation of Shirazi's theory of Islamic rule as a method, beginning from the top, we would find it as follows: -

1. An Islamic system of government is fundamental
2. The leadership of this system can either be headed by a single individual (Wilayat Faqih) or by a collective body of religious authorities that satisfy the required criteria (leadership council of religious authorities).
3. In the case of the leadership council, the collective body may choose one of them as the leader, or agree to make rule a consultative process amongst them.
4. Both the individual leadership and the Leadership Council for Religious Authority are decided according to direct election or through elected deputies, to be elected for this particular purpose.

Shirazi believes in "council of religious authorities" as a special theory, but he makes its implementation conditional on the nation's approval, for elections to him are a fundamental principle that can be neither breached nor superseded.

Evidence of Shura (Collective Leadership) and the Final Picture

The crux of Shirazi's theory of "council of religious authorities" is that it should be the people's choice. But why? The answer is simple. The evidence available leads him to adopt this form of leadership in Islam. Some of the evidence he quote is:

1. In Qur'anic Verse: *"Their affairs are (solved on) consultation amongst them"*; and the Verse *"Consult them on the matter"*.

2. In principle Allah has not appointed a religious authority to rule. Therefore this leads to the conclusion that any one of them may be elected to rule.

3. "Imam Sadiq (PBUH) is quoted to say to companions: be aware, if a dispute breaks up amongst them, or if an argument ensues, never to put the matter to any of those corrupts. Appoint from your ranks a man who knows our *halaal* (what is allowed) and *haraam* (what is forbidden). For, I have appointed such man a judge. But never take one another to the (judges of) a tyrant unjust ruler."

4. "Imam Sadiq (PBUH) is quoted to say "Look for that amongst you who has narrated and quoted our Teachings and understood our *halaal* and *haraam*, and known our laws and rules makes him an arbiter, for I have appointed him a ruler".

Shirazi lists a total of nineteen statements of evidence, which he draws from the Qur'an, the Sunnah, the consensus, and reason. He then investigates the points of doubt raised on the concept of Shura, and refutes them one after another.

It seems to me that this evidential exposition of the theory of "council of religious authorities" can be easily concluded with this finale`:

"The basic component of the Islamic government is "council of religious authorities"; for these authorities are the representatives of the Imams (PBUT), whom are in turn the appointed rulers and successors (of the prophet). The prophet (PBUH) says, "O god, have mercy on my successors"; and Sadiq (PBUH) says, "For I have appointed such man a ruler". There is no justification to make some religious authority rulers, and exclude others, for that amount to a removal of the messenger's successor and the ruler appointed by the Imam. It is not right to say that religious authority does not understand or comprehend, or to make (similar accusations); if such a religious authority has been willingly accepted by the majority of the Muslim Community, he must become a partner and a party in ruling (the Muslim State)."[132]

---

[132] M. Shirazi, "How to Unite the Muslims", p18

Elections and their Problems

Election is a very important aspect in Shirazi's theory of leadership in Islam. That is why he did not allow it to float uncontrolled. He establishes it on strong Islamic principles and regulates it as follows: -

1- Leadership will be effected through free elections. The head of state must be the choice of the majority of the people, provided that he meets the set criteria and possesses the qualifications ordained by Allah, like probity, justice and expertise in matters of faith, and knowledge of worldly affairs."[133] This is the fundamental principle.

2- Such elections should not be ceremonial, but a reality in which all people participate. Rallies and telegrams of support are not elections, only voting is.

3- Yet such elections are not a pre-condition to appoint the head of state, but also to appoint the regional or local governors; "... In every region and district of the Muslim country, people must elect a religious authority to be their governor. Those regional governors must submit to the head of state, who is also elected by the majority of the Community"[134]

4- It is necessary to hold general elections from time to time, say once every four or five years - to choose head of the state and other local governors, all to be chosen by majority of vote."[135]

Shirazi is not oblivious to criticism and point of doubt raised against elections and Shura (Collective System of Leadership). Often sharp criticisms of these two political concepts are made, and are alleged to be near impossible to implement.

The main criticism against elections centres on the possibility of manipulation of results.

---

[133] M. Shirazi, "The Way to Muslim Revival", p 22

[134] ibid.

[135] ibid.

Another is that the danger of the chance of winning the elections by majority vote depends on the candidate's financial, publicity and support capabilities, which may vary from one candidate to another.

It is no secret that suspicions are due to the bitter experiences of the election process, whether in so-called free countries or third world countries. In the latter, elections are a scandalous farce, created by a diversity of factors, mostly cheating, forgery and lies, not only by presidents and rulers, but even by small officials. This has bred frustration in the heart of nations and peoples towards elections, despite the fact that, as an idea and a sacred method in the conscience, elections are very desirable, even a wish, a dear one, for they are logical and appeals strongly to instinct.

However, we do not wish to tackle the issue of elections in the language of reason. For, not everything that is liable to fiddling must be rejected. Such a method would paralyse all life energies, thus opening the doors for the logic of death and inaptitude to dominate the whole existence.

Nor do we wish to say that such criticism and points of doubt do not exist in Muslim societies, even in very small degrees, due to general education practised in these societies, which are based on piety, honesty, sincerity and courage.

It is true that all these critical issues, essential should not hamper us as they are, but there is a very important issue alluded to by Shirazi in this respect, i.e., awareness and education. The spread of education and awareness amongst the public is bound to deter such shortcomings. According to him, education breeds awareness, which in turn deters fraud, forgery, fiddling, putting-off, and foul play.

Yet all of this is subject to experiment; the more experimentation, the more mature people and nations become. Thus they can tackle the first and second dirty tricks. Experience is the factory of nations and people.

The above-mentioned criticism is a fact, but solving it is not impossible. It may be difficult but should not be yielded to. Awareness and experience guarantee the solving of this problem.

Dilemma of the Majority Concept

Ayatollah Shirazi further outlines the criticism and doubts thrown at the concept of "Majority". These can be summered up as follows:

1. That Allah the Almighty has dispraised the majority: *"If you obeyed the majority of those on Earth, they would mislead you away from the path of Allah"*.

2. Giving the whole nation the right to vote entails equality between the learned (literate) and the ignorant (illiterate).

3. The majority might be a minority. For example in an election with three candidates the election results may turn out to be 35%, 33% and 32% respectively. To opt for the majority in this case means that, for the majority of thirty five, we are in fact ignoring the votes of sixty five".

4. The rule of the majority may liquidate the minority.

Shirazi deals with all these criticisms, logically, objectively and clearly:

As for the fact that the Qur'an dispraised the majority, this is not without qualifications, but it applies only to times when the majority deviate from the straight path of Allah.

The consequent equality of the literate and illiterate is meant to be at the level of the general and common right. It is therefore neither unjust nor harmful.

The third criticism laid against the majority is untrue, because the majority has accepted the method. Moreover, its entitlement to consultation and support is justifiable. In any case favouring the majority is a basic equipment of consultation stipulated in Qur'an, the Sunnah (the Teaching of the Prophet), reason and consensus.

The forth point can be refuted according to the third answer, i.e., the right of majority can not be nullified... It is after all, a matter of what is important and what is more important. [136]

Council of Religious Authority Faces Two Problems

The Council of Religious Authority has two problems to tackle and solve:

1. The emergence of the difference of verdicts or judgement of a religious authority with that of the leadership council of religious authority.
2. How to bring together all the religious authority in one council when they are located in various countries.

Shirazi's answer to the first problem is that "...the apparent ruling is that the follower should follow the verdict of the council (of religious authorities). This is similar to the case of the individual who needs to make a choice between the opinion of his own religious mentor and that of a judge - should a case of dispute be referred to the judge. It has been concluded that in such cases the opinion of the judge must be adopted."[137] For this case Shirazi draws from two evidential references:

1. the duty of a judge (in Islamic tradition)
2. References, as in "*Nahj_ul_Balaghah*", which stipulate that "*Shura* is the right of the Immigrants and Partisans if they agree on one man and value him as an leader, that would be pleasing to Allah. If one of them deviates from the nation, whether by defaming or creating an innovation, they should bring him back to the ranks. If he refuses, they should fight him for his deviation from the path of the believers"[138]

The answer to the second problem is included in this following statement by Shirazi:

---

[136]M. Shirazi, *al-Fiqh* series, volume 99, "Government in Islam", case 4, p 56

[137] M. Shirazi, *al-Fiqh* series, volume 105, Politics, p 271

[138] ibid., p 272

"... It is possible to have their representatives in one council, who will convey their respective points of view to the council, and, in turn, report back to them. Decisions are arrived at by majority vote." [139]

Qualifications of the Muslim Ruler

Shirazi is in agreement with most religious scholars as to the qualifications and qualities of the Muslim ruler and conditions he should meet. They are:

1. Adolescence
2. Sound mind
3. Faith
4. Expertise
5. Complete probity and justice
6. Purity of birth
7. Life (Alive)
8. Male gender. [140]

Scholarly superiority is not the condition, which is the opinion of the majority of scholars, like the authors of Masalik and Jawahir. As for courage, generosity and indifference to worldly pleasures... those are additional qualities, which add points to the eligibility and priority of a certain candidate. [141]

Important Remarks

1- Electing the religious authorities to power does not strip them of their traditional post and duties (as religious authorities). [142]

---

[139] M. Shirazi, "How to Unite the Muslims", p 20

[140] M. Shirazi, *al-Fiqh* series, volume 105, Politics, p 282

[141] ibid., p 286

[142] ibid., p 271

2- If a religious authority loses the required qualities and therefore his fitness for the post, i.e. He comes to suffer from symptoms that invalidate him as such, he loses his right to rule.[143]

3- It is necessary to hold general elections from time to time, say once every four or five years, to choose the head of state and regional governors, in accordance with the vote of the majority.[144]

4- A head of state whether an individual or collective, must ensure that they consult others on various others. The advisors must have five main qualities:

1. A sound mind
2. Freedom
3. Piety
4. Honesty
5. Expertise in the field.

General Conclusion

If we study Ayatollah Shirazi's theory of Islam deeply, we find it centred on two essential points:

1- Collective Leadership
2- Elections

He remarkably combines these two aspects, showing great consideration for scholarship on the one hand and the rights of the nation on the other. He also shows a great consideration for the innate fundamental nature of freedom, which he deeply believes in and very strongly advocates. He in fact strikes a tight dialectic relationship between freedom and justice.

Collective leadership is the ideal form of Islamic rule according to Shirazi, but not through enforced oppressive imposition; only as a result of the free choice of the nation, thus stressing the concept of elections, which necessitates freedom and justice simultaneously. He is deeply honest and self-consistent, and consistent with the others when he states that if the nation chooses one of its religious authorities as the head of state, it is free to do so, and it may not be prevented from doing so.

---

[143] M. Shirazi, "How to Unite the Muslims", p 20

[144] M. Shirazi, "The Way to Muslim Revival", p 22

Shirazi's theory shows a great respect for the mind and the free will; it is also consistent with mankind's aspiration to be a party to the process of deciding his own destiny. It is no exaggeration to say that adopting this theory, taking into consideration its above - mentioned courses, would provide the right atmosphere and climate to develop popular will and free conscience.

A Quick Comparative Look

It is not any exaggerations if we stated here that adopting other than collective leadership may lead to individual dictatorship, even if inadvertently. Some of the factors, which support this view, are: -

1. The power and the authority of the as head of state, just like the powers of the Infallible Imams are great and wide.
2. There would be no consultation with others even if all the religious scholars (Faqihs) were equal in rank and expertise.
3. The Head of State is not required, in this case, to consult or seek the advice of prominent scholars, or the people.
4. Every Faqih who meets all the conditions has the right to power and authority. As this leads to chaos and confusion, this power or authority should be confined to one (Faqih only) to be chosen by the nation!
5. The head of state has authority over other Faqihs and their followers.
6. If differences of opinion emerge between the head of state and another religious scholar, the head of state has the final word on the matters of rulings and other subjects.
7. Finally, the whole body of religious authorities should be in the grip of the head of state.

I do not wish to comment on these propositions from a juristic point of view; for, I am not a religious scholar. I would only look at the general atmosphere, which those propositions may create and lead to.

It is undoubtedly an atmosphere abundant with force and apprehension, and it creates a state of non-compatibility between the people and the Islamic government, and spreads discord within the institutions of religious authorities.

Statements quoted in the following passage go against all that the Shi'a school of thought came to be known as over the past ages. "...The prohibition of the multiplicity of religious authorities, whether the Faqih was a ruler enjoying a free hand in government, or with restricted and limited powers, isolated from the field of effective action. For, whatever the reason behind this distance from leadership, such a Faqih - ruler has no right to allow multiplicity of religious authorities or institutions...."[145].

Shirazi's theory comes closer to Sadr's in this respect. Sadr advocates individual Faqih as head of state, but not in the sense of the frightening example introduced in the above paragraphs.

Sadr is of the opinion that the religious authority (Faqih) who accepts the challenge and stands up to this task is the effective leader. However, "he must form a council composed of a hundred of the best scholars from at Shi'a religious colleges, representatives of other religious authorities, scholars, speakers, authors, and intellectuals. At least ten religious scholars must be members of the council. The institution of religious authorities will then function through the said Council."[146]

In other cases, when the normal process of entrusting (someone) in charge (of the government) does not arise, for example, when certain events lead to the formation of an Islamic government (a sudden popular revolution, or a military coup which decides to adopt Islamic rule), a Faqih would then come to power. He should be nominated by "the majority of the members of the Council of religious authorities, and seconded by a large number of religious activists, and should include scholars, students of religious colleges, scholars' representatives, mosque leaders, public speakers, and Islamic intellectuals."[147] The candidate should, however, meet the set requirement for this post, like expertise, justice, and probity; and should have a clear Islamic line of thought, expressed in his books and publications.

---

[145] A.M. Muhanna, "Islamic Government"

[146] M.B. Sadr, "Islam Leads the Way"

[147] ibid.

He should be a religious authority of the community, which he must attain by known normal methods.[148] And, "in the case of multiplicity of equally qualified religious authorities, the public must choose the head of state by general elections"

Sadr, therefore, advocates leadership of religious authority, but only through elections and implementation of the consultation system. The latter being of high effectiveness in the administration of the state as long as the religious authority functions through consultation system, according to Sadr.

There is some sort of concurrence in opinion as to the importance of the community's opinion. In any case in his theory of Islamic rule, Shirazi has achieved the following results:

1. Implementation of Allah's Law through the choice of the people,
2. Maintaining the dignity of the religious authority institution, and safeguarding its right to take charge of the government,
3. Activating political awareness of the nation,
4. Protecting the unity of the people against division and discord.

---

[148] ibid.